EXPLORING NORFOLK'S

DEEP HISTORY COAST

T0333523

JOHN A. DAVIES
DAVID M.G. WATERHOUSE

The History Press

First published 2023

The History Press
97 St George's Place, Cheltenham,
Gloucestershire, GL50 3QB
www.thehistorypress.co.uk

British Library Cataloguing in Publication Data.
A catalogue record for this book is available from the British Library.

ISBN 978 1 80399 171 9

Typesetting and origination by The History Press
Printed and bound in Great Britain by TJ Books Limited, Padstow, Cornwall.

Trees for L Y fe

CONTENTS

About the Authors   4
Acknowledgements   6
Illustration Credits   7
Foreword   8
Introduction   10

1 An Introduction to Norfolk's Deep History Coast   13
2 The Natural Setting   23
3 The Geology   32
4 The Changing Fauna   50
5 The First Humans   65
6 The East: Pakefield to West Runton   75
7 The Central North Coast: Sheringham to Holme   107
8 The West: Hunstanton to the Wash   131
9 Accessing and Learning from the Deep History Coast   148

Glossary   164
Further Reading   166

ABOUT THE AUTHORS

DR JOHN A. DAVIES was Chief Curator for Norfolk Museums Service (NMS), member of the senior management team and Keeper of Archaeology until December 2018. Prior to retiring, he was Project Director (at NMS) for the major project to redevelop the historic Norman keep at Norwich Castle – the largest museum heritage project in the UK. He previously led the Interreg European project 'Norman Connections', linking historic sites in Normandy and southern England. He has worked as an archaeologist in Norfolk since 1984 and is a highly experienced museum professional of over thirty years. His publications include *The Land of Boudica: Prehistoric and Roman Norfolk* (2009), *Castles in the Anglo-Norman World* (2015), *A History of Norfolk in 100 Objects* (2015) and *The Little History of Norfolk* (2020). He is a Fellow of the Society of Antiquaries.

DR DAVID M.G. WATERHOUSE is a palaeontologist, evolutionary biologist and illustrator. He is the Curator of the Polar Museum at the Scott Polar Research Institute, University of Cambridge. Until early 2023 he spent sixteen years at Norfolk Museums Service (NMS), where he was Senior Curator of Natural History and Geology (responsible for the museums' natural science collections from gnats to mammoths – and everything in between!). He is a former General Secretary of the Geological Society of Norfolk, a founder member of Norfolk Geodiversity Partnership, and a steering group member of the nationally acclaimed Norwich Science Festival. He was lead author and editor of *The Wonder of Birds: Nature, Art, Culture* (2014). David's excavation experience includes the oldest archaeological site in northern Europe at Happisburgh in Norfolk, a complete ichthyosaur in Whitby, North Yorkshire, and a *Tyrannosaurus rex* dig in Montana, USA.

ACKNOWLEDGEMENTS

The authors would like to thank those who have willingly shared with us their knowledge of Norfolk's landscape, geology, ancient fauna, early archaeology and information about specific discoveries, as well as their inspiration, over many years. In particular, and in alphabetical order, these are: Nick Ashton, Beau Brannick, Mike Chambers, the late Harold and Margaret Hems, the late Peter Hoare, Tony Irwin, Nigel Larkin, Simon Lewis, Jenny Lyon, Simon Parfitt, the late Peter Robins, Tony Stuart, Martin Warren and the late John Wymer.

The support and continued encouragement provided by Nick Ashton, Simon Lewis, Simon Parfitt, Chris Stringer and all members of the Ancient Human Occupation of Britain (AHOB) project team and the Pathways to Ancient Britain project team has always been gratefully appreciated.

We would also like to acknowledge the contributions of the many amateur enthusiasts who have shared information from their collections and those who have submitted their finds to NMS for identification and recording. They are too numerous to mention individually.

The idea of Deep History Coast was created and developed through our curatorial roles at NMS. The authors would like to thank all our friends and colleagues at NMS who have actively supported the project. The initiative has been progressed in partnership with North Norfolk District Council, who we would also like to thank for its involvement and support.

We hope that the project will serve to emphasise the importance of the role of museums and their staff in relation to the understanding of the county's natural and historic heritage and the importance of wider community engagement towards its interpretation and preservation.

ILLUSTRATION CREDITS

FOREWORD

The delicate nature of Norfolk's fragile coast has been further highlighted since the submission of our book for publication. The rate of erosion along the eastern seaboard has accelerated alarmingly in recent months. In February 2023 the small village of Hemsby hit national headlines when it lost 3m of coastline to the sea in just two days. Then, during the spring high tide in March, it was losing 3m in a single day. It became necessary for the beach to be sealed off beneath the unstable cliffs and properties were evacuated in advance of their destruction.

The causes of such catastrophes are complex, but changes around the east coast have become visible, with the build-up of sand banks alongside intensified erosion in other places. There is no question that the threat to parts of our coastline has become acute. Prior to the extreme weather conditions of 2018, which were referred to as 'The Beast from the East', erosion on this part of the coast was measured at around 1m per year. We are now seeing more extreme weather conditions on a regular basis, with what were once simply natural processes now being accelerated by the current climate crisis.

It is hoped that this book will serve to help raise awareness of the threat to some of our more delicate natural coastal habitats and their flora and fauna. Coastal communities, together with their homes and infrastructure, will continue to be at risk. The cycle of change is becoming more rapid.

Norfolk's Deep History Coast remains a magical and dynamic place to visit. Most recently, Gorleston beach, with its stunning bay, has been included in the list of Europe's twenty-five top beaches for 2023. It was also named the best beach in the

UK. Here, we look to celebrate the beauty and significance of this historic coastline and to encourage your enjoyment and participation in its preservation.

John Davies and David Waterhouse
April 2023

INTRODUCTION

Some of the biggest and most fascinating questions of our time are those concerning who we are and where we came from. Now, in the twenty-first century, we are living through uncertain times for the human race, facing threats to the survival of our species in the form of global warming, pandemics and political instability, and all in the context of the threat of a sixth major extinction of life on the planet. Scientists are warning that our climate is currently at its warmest level since before the last ice age, some 125,000 years ago. Now may be an appropriate time to look back into distant deep time, from where we can regard a great panorama of past events in earth's long journey and learn from it.

Our world has already undergone periods of climate change. Throughout history, human populations have been faced with problems relating to migration and displacement of peoples, ethnicity and identity. Yet, our species has survived, and we may be able to learn lessons from those who have gone before us.

So why is it that such massive issues are of relevance to Norfolk and, in particular, to its coastline? The answer is that past changes to the environment and climate, which have had a direct influence on the survival of the human species and the peopling of the earth, can be observed in the geology and archaeology that is being revealed in this county. In Norfolk, we are discovering important new clues to these events along the coastline, which is undergoing change brought about by a combination of natural forces, some of which have been accelerated by human action. Evidence here is also being uncovered that is able to shed new light on the very earliest human occupation of Europe and the delicate relationship our species has maintained with the natural landscape. The leading palaeontologist Professor Richard Fortey has described this part of Britain as 'a fragile part of the country' and 'a place to feel the ephemeral grasp we have on the past' (1993).

In recent decades, science has steadily made us aware of massive, submerged lost land masses around Great Britain and their significance to human occupation and survival. We now know that it was as recently as just 8,500 years ago that Britain was physically joined to mainland Europe. Archaeologists are currently investigating how and when areas of former dry land situated beyond Norfolk's present coastline were drowned and are mapping these vast, hidden landscapes. There is now worldwide interest in drowned landscapes and coastal archaeology. Norfolk's coastline is becoming a focal point in these studies.

From this approach, and from the emerging evidence on Norfolk's coast, we can begin to understand how planetary processes and climate change have shaped the human story. We may also ask what other species we have shared the earth with and why so many of them are no longer with us. These are enormous questions and the study of Norfolk's coastline is helping to provide some of the answers.

So, Norfolk's geography and coastal geology are revealing unique vital clues to the earliest history of the human species and its natural environment. In this short introduction to what we have called 'Deep History Coast', we shall look at these discoveries and their significance, and also explain how you can become involved in this great adventure.

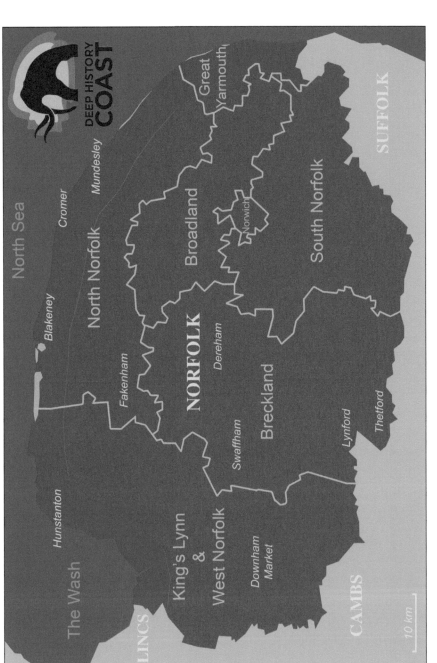

Fig. 1: The extent of Norfolk's Deep History Coast.

1. AN INTRODUCTION TO NORFOLK'S DEEP HISTORY COAST

INTRODUCTION

The Deep History Coast is a part of England's eastern seaboard, located where the land mass of the British Isles projects outward into the North Sea. Situated on the fringes of the county of Norfolk, where sea meets land, this is where some of the country's most spectacular archaeological discoveries have been made. Here, it is possible to experience some of the most significant archaeological sites in the whole of Europe; all located within the most beautiful natural settings. Visitors can enjoy a range of natural habitats, open countryside and pretty villages, together with local museums and other attractions, along the county's extensive coastline.

People are already attracted to this part of the country for recreation: to enjoy the unspoiled natural beauty of its beaches, the wildlife, a leisurely country stroll or bike ride, a meal in a scenic restaurant or fish and chips by the seaside. But few are fully aware of the aspects related to Norfolk's history, less so, its very earliest past. Most people would be amazed to know that discoveries along Norfolk's coast in recent decades show this apparently quiet and rural part of the country to have been the cradle of humankind for the whole of north-west Europe. And these discoveries continue to be made.

DISCOVERIES ALONG THE COAST

It has long been suspected that there had been an extremely early human presence on and close to what is now the coast of Norfolk. Early flint tools made by our ancient relatives have been found on the county's beaches since the mid-nineteenth century. Here, early multipurpose prehistoric tools called handaxes (see glossary, page 164) have been discovered regularly. These objects tend to be worn and rounded from having been rolled in the sea and on sandy beaches for very long periods. It is also likely that some may have travelled from their original locations by the process of coastal drift.

Fig. 2: A Lower Palaeolithic flint handaxe found on Eccles beach in 2004. It is considered to be in excess of 500,000 years old.

Although they often lack association with dateable geological deposits, archaeologists regard these tools as an indicator of very early activity along and in the vicinity of Norfolk's coast. But just how old are they? Other discoveries are now indicating that they may date to times long before what has previously been considered possible.

Interest in the earliest history of Norfolk's coast was stimulated by a spectacular discovery during the winter of 1990. Following a storm, enormous bones were exposed in a cliff at West Runton, to the west of Cromer, which were later identified as those of a male mammoth, belonging to the species popularly known as the steppe mammoth.

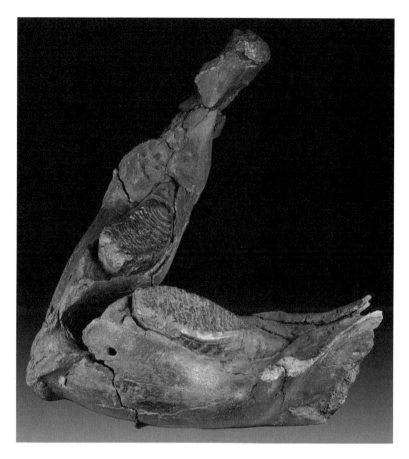

Fig. 3: The huge jaw of the West Runton mammoth, which lived about 700,000 years ago.

This was probably the largest species of mammoth that ever lived. The creature was much larger and double the weight of the biggest elephant living today. The skeleton of the West Runton mammoth is now one of the county's most important and iconic specimens. This important discovery served to focus the attention of both amateurs and professionals towards the importance of the north Norfolk coast for fossil discoveries, which have continued to be made.

Just a few years later, in the year 2000, Simon Parfitt, working at the Natural History Museum and University College London, recognised some distinctive marks in the bone of a very ancient prehistoric bison that had been found at Happisburgh, on the coast of north-east Norfolk. These were made by cuts from a flint tool, proving that very early humans had been present in the vicinity when the bison is known to have died, about 500,000 years ago. In the same year, local beachcomber Mike Chambers was walking on Happisburgh beach when he saw an object poking up from the surface of a peaty sediment on the wave line. This turned out to be a perfectly complete prehistoric handaxe. Not only was it in fresher condition than the other handaxes previously found on the Norfolk coast but it had also been found in situ, within a secure geological deposit, which is now also dated to about half a million years ago. As a result of these two discoveries, archaeological excavations were subsequently undertaken at Happisburgh, which led to the discovery of an even earlier human presence.

Another significant discovery associated with the presence of early humans on and close to the coast of Norfolk can be traced further back, to 1931, when a block of peat was dredged up a from the seabed beyond Cromer containing a beautiful polished, barbed harpoon made from red-deer antler. It was recognised that this weapon had been used by a prehistoric hunter. The peat around it had been formed in freshwater conditions, proving that this location had once been inland from the sea.

Fig. 4: The Happisburgh handaxe, discovered in 2000. It has been dated to approximately 500,000 years ago.

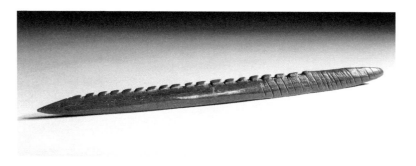

Fig. 5: The exquisite, polished antler harpoon found in peat from the seabed beyond Cromer, in 1931. It was used and lost about 12,000 years ago.

Radiocarbon dating subsequently showed that this area of peat had been formed about 12,000 years ago and the spearhead had been used by people at the end of the last ice age. It proved that a substantial area of dry land had once continued beyond the present Norfolk coastline and parts of the North Sea had provided a 'land bridge' to and from other parts of Europe. This discovery served to focus research into the exploration of a lost landscape and, ultimately, the concept of climate change, which continues as a major subject of study today.

Important archaeological discoveries have continued to be made on Norfolk's coast and they are not restricted to just the very earliest episodes of our prehistory. In 1998, John Lorimer was walking on the beach at Holme dunes, in the far north-west, when he made the amazing discovery of a large, inverted tree trunk sticking up above the sand. This was found to be set within an oval-shaped wooden enclosure. This intriguing structure quickly became known by the popular name of Seahenge. Modern scientific techniques enabled it to be dated very precisely to 2049 BC, which was during the Bronze Age.

Fig. 6: The timber circle known as Seahenge, discovered in 1998. It was constructed over 4,000 years ago. It is no longer present on Holme beach.

Such discoveries continue to capture the attention and imagination of everybody interested in our human past. Norfolk's beautiful coastline and its adjacent countryside have proven to be exceptionally rich in significant archaeological and palaeontological discoveries, which are important to the national and international, as well as our local, story. Together, they cause us to pose new questions and to rewrite the story of humankind. This all deserves to be better known. Norfolk's Deep History Coast serves to provide an important opportunity, allowing us to better understand our ancient and most distant human origins.

THE SIGNIFICANCE OF NORFOLK'S COASTLINE

The prehistory and subsequent historical development of Norfolk are inextricably linked with its extensive coastline, which stretches for some 150km through varied scenery, embracing stretches of cliffs, beautiful golden sandy beaches and marshland.

This entire coast provides wonderful places to visit and stay for holidays. It is also a great location to observe wildlife, especially its variety of birds, many of which make landfall on their migrations between Scandinavia and the rest of Europe.

For thousands of years, this coast has been integral to the character of the area's inhabitants, as a source of their livelihood and prosperity. In more recent historical times, fishing ports were located at regular intervals, from Great Yarmouth in the east, through Cromer and the Glaven ports in the north, to King's Lynn in the west. Such important locations would undoubtedly have been exploited at earlier times too, including in the Roman period (see Chapters 6 and 7). Strong cultural and trading links were forged with other parts of Europe and worldwide, and agricultural produce from inland was exported from here to other parts of Britain and the Continent.

But this is a coastline that also suffers from its exposed location, especially from strong seasonal gales and storms. The east coast, in particular, is highly unstable and prone to flooding and reclamation by the sea. In 1604, the entire village of Eccles was lost to the sea. Today, this is the fastest-receding coastline in the whole of Europe.

Although prevailing weather conditions sometimes pose an alarming threat to coastal communities and farmland, the resulting erosion has been responsible for a series of outstanding archaeological and palaeontological discoveries. Norfolk's fascinating and internationally recognised geology is being eroded to reveal finds of the highest significance, which illustrate aspects of its past, providing evidence for some of the very earliest humans to enter Europe, as well as its ancient fauna.

The foreshore at Happisburgh revealed the oldest archaeological site in northern Europe, while the beach at West Runton yielded the largest and oldest nearly complete mammoth skeleton ever found in the British Isles. Norfolk now has evidence for more species of humans than any other county in the country. In fact, finds from this coast have been vital in helping us to understand just how the story of Britain began.

These discoveries have not only transformed our understanding of Britain's earliest prehistory but also contributed to a much bigger story. They yield an insight into the very earliest human presence, occupation and settlement of Europe.

In addition to its lengthy coastline, Norfolk is also separated from the rest of Britain by water. While contained by sea to the north and east, today's county is separated from Suffolk and Cambridgeshire in the south by the Little Ouse and Waveney rivers. To the west, situated between Norfolk and the English Midlands, are the watery expanses of the Wash and the fenland. The area comprising the modern county of Norfolk is, in effect, surrounded by water, creating almost an island.

THE IDEA OF DEEP HISTORY – WHEN WAS IT?

In this book, we shall consider the early history of humankind and the integral relationship between geology and the natural environment from the evidence being revealed in Norfolk. In order to do so, we need to understand the concept of very distant time. When we are looking at the transformation of the earth, it is almost impossible to comprehend the hundreds of millions of years in question. Human presence on the earth is relatively recent in such a context but still involves millions of years. The established terminology used by archaeologists has not been helpful.

The labels used to describe very early human times can be confusing to the non-specialist. The term 'prehistory' is a word that was first used in the early 1800s to describe the time before writing was invented. It literally means 'before history', although this is confusing because events were already happening, even if no one was writing about them. In different cultures and regions of the world, writing began at different times, so 'prehistory' isn't even a fixed point in time across the globe.

It was during the nineteenth century that the study of prehistory was first structured on what were considered to be the predominant technologies used for the production of objects. Unfortunately, the terms 'Stone Age', 'Bronze Age' and 'Iron Age' have remained in use, although their significance has long been discredited and recognised as somewhat misleading. Archaeology in the twentieth century has constructed a more sophisticated interpretation of the past, which reveals a far more complex narrative, in which there were more significant developments in society than those simply based on the use of particular materials at different times.

Today, the Stone Age period is subdivided into the Palaeolithic, Mesolithic and Neolithic. These labels are also often explained as meaning the Old Stone Age, Middle Stone Age and New Stone Age. Even so, the terms still convey very little to most people.

The more attractive concept of Deep Time has become increasingly used to describe the very long expanses of time in relation to the development of the earth, and this covers the enormous periods when the sediments and rocks around us were being formed. The term was first used in the early 1980s, specifically in relation to the processes involved in geology. More recently, the term Deep History has been introduced and relates to the part of Deep Time when humans existed.

Deep History as a concept applies to humankind's most distant past – to the beginnings of humankind. It is mainly to the years of Deep History that this book will be dedicated, although some significant episodes further back into Deep Time will also be considered, as well as some more recent periods when appropriate, in order to provide a fuller context for our exploration.

THE CONCEPT OF DEEP HISTORY COAST

The increase in knowledge of our early human past comes from new sources. The processes of archaeological and geological study in Norfolk are now aided by accelerating coastal erosion alongside interventions by the offshore energy industry and gravel extraction, all of which reveal new sites of interest and significance. Archaeology is also assisted by deep-sea surveying methods and sensitive new scientific dating techniques.

The archaeological and palaeontological discoveries in Norfolk, referred to in this chapter, involving both early human remains and spectacular giant fauna, relate to very early times and have shown the relevance of the term 'Deep History' to the county's lengthy coast. This important coastline and its unique geology continues to reveal important information associated with the earliest humans in Britain. In this book, we shall tour Norfolk's coast, looking at sites and discoveries, and undertake a survey of the county's distant past. It was from the growing appreciation of the importance of Norfolk's coastal finds that we developed the concept and title 'Deep History Coast'.

Today, we are becoming increasingly aware of the issues of climate change, the depletion of species and destruction of the natural world around us. The study of Norfolk's geology and archaeological record have a relevance to major global issues and threats that are facing humankind in the twenty-first century. Their study provides evidence of the effects of previous climate change and the extinction of species. The discoveries related to early humans provide clues as to when and why our distant ancestors moved around the world.

In later chapters we shall follow the coastline, from the extreme south-east, at the border with Suffolk, progressing north and then westward, looking at relevant sites, coastal features, landscape and geology. We shall see that there is, in fact, a broad chronological logic to surveying Norfolk's coast in an anticlockwise fashion in this way.

Most of our exploration of the Deep History Coast will focus on the earliest habitation of the area and its exploitation. While providing an introduction to aspects relating to very early Deep History, we shall also explore some other historic sites and look more broadly at periods of early history, as well as prehistory, as they are logically revealed along the coastline. But first, we shall take a closer look at the importance of the earth's natural changes and their impact on the evolution of humankind and its spread across the world.

2. THE NATURAL SETTING

AN INTRODUCTION TO THE WORLD OF DEEP TIME

In this chapter, we shall consider how the earth's evolutionary forces gave rise to the dynamic conditions from which the origins and development of the human story began. Our planet was formed 4.5 billion years ago and it remains in a constantly changing state. It was these natural forces and processes that drove the planet towards the period that we call Deep History.

The earth's solid outer layer (the crust) is made up from a number of enormous rocky plates and the study of their interaction is called plate tectonics. These plates are in a continuous state of movement and, where they come together, massive forces are released. It is at these locations that a number of the world's most remarkable geological features have been formed. These include such formations as the Himalayan mountain range and, of particular relevance to our current story, the great East African Rift Valley. Plate tectonics were the cause of the major changes that forged the geology and environments that enabled the development of life as we know it today.

The earth's climate has also been subject to continuous change and fluctuation. Over the last 50 million years, the world's climate has undergone a steady cooling process. These processes were responsible for some of the major extinction events that occurred on five previous occasions, which will be considered separately in Chapter 4.

Tectonics created the conditions that ultimately resulted in the evolution of the human species. About 30 million years ago, the action of plate tectonics released the hot mantle upwards from beneath the earth's crust, forcing the land apart and creating the great Rift Valley and the diverse environment of East Africa, in which we evolved as a family. Over time, the region experienced a decline in rainfall and forest was replaced with the open grassland of the savannah. It was this development, in particular, which stimulated the evolution of humans from tree-dwelling apes.

About 2.6 million years ago, the earth entered a new epoch called the Pleistocene, which was characterised by a recurring cycle of ice ages. Norfolk, along with the rest of East Anglia, contains the fullest evidence for the Pleistocene in the whole of Britain. These events comprised a series of cold periods, or glaciations, which were separated by episodes when the climate became warmer. As the ice sheets expanded and then receded, so sea levels fell and rose, resulting in actions that sculpted the landscape and altered the courses of rivers.

The landscape of Norfolk that we see today was formed by the action of ice, both in the form of direct physical impact of the ice sheets and in the sediments that were deposited at their margins through outwash from the glaciers and accumulations of gravels. They left rich and fertile deposits of silt, clay and beds of loam, which created the conditions that have provided us with today's rich agricultural land.

ERA	PERIOD	EPOCH	YEARS AGO	EVENTS
CENOZOIC	Quaternary	Holocene		Current interglacial
CENOZOIC	Quaternary	Pleistocene	11,000	
CENOZOIC	Neogene	Pliocene	2.6 million	Origin of genus *Homo*
CENOZOIC	Neogene	Miocene	5.3 million	Onset of Ice Ages Origin of hominins
CENOZOIC	Palaeogene	Oligocene	23 million	East African Rift formed
CENOZOIC	Palaeogene	Eocene	34 million	Chilling of climate
CENOZOIC	Palaeogene	Palaeocene	56 million	The age of mammals
MESOZOIC	Cretaceous	Upper	66 million	5th mass extinction Dinosaurs living

Fig. 7: Timeline of geological events.

THE AGE OF ICE

The Ice Age comprised a series of successive glaciations, which are known as the Beestonian, Anglian, Wolstonian and Devensian glaciations. Between them were warm periods known as interglacials. We have evidence for human presence at stages throughout the Ice Age, although it was a sporadic rather than a continuous presence.

The Beestonian Glaciation

From 1.8 million years ago, this was the first major phase of glaciation during the early Pleistocene. It is named after Norfolk's Beeston cliffs, which are situated near West Runton. It led into the Cromerian stage.

The Cromerian Interglacial

The period from 900,000–500,000 years ago covered the geological warm stage known as the Cromerian. During this interglacial (named after the type-site near Cromer on the north coast) Norfolk was covered by temperate forest, which stretched all the way to the European mainland across what is now the North Sea.

Our evidence for human activity at that time is increasing steadily. Unfortunately, no human skeletal remains have been found for this very early period in Norfolk; neither do we have evidence for dwellings or other structures from this early time. People would probably have made shelters from simple hide-covered constructions, perhaps made from wood or even from the bones of large mammals.

The Anglian Glaciation

The onset of the Anglian Cold Stage (500,000–424,000 years ago) saw major glaciation affect the whole of East Anglia, and Norfolk was covered in a thick sheet of ice, which extended south almost as far as Clacton and Thurrock, in Essex. This was to have a major effect on the earlier river systems. It destroyed the Bytham River (see the following section concerning drainage).

There were some ice-free intervals during the Anglian stage, during which the vegetation was mainly grasses and sedges. Finds from across Britain show that there were regular visits from humans during some warmer phases but evidence for hunters in Norfolk becomes more common during the Late Anglian Stage. Their flint tools have been found at sites including Weybourne, Runton, Sidestrand, Mundesley, Bacton and Lessingham. Coastal locations have also produced Palaeolithic flints in the vicinity of Anglian glacial deposits at Cley-next-the-Sea, Overstrand, Paston, Sea Palling and Happisburgh.

The Hoxnian Interglacial

The Hoxnian Interglacial (424,000–370,000 years ago) was characterised by a mild oceanic climate and saw the reappearance of temperate vegetation and animals. By the middle of this period, there was an expansion of hunter-gatherer presence across East Anglia and Britain in general.

The Wolstonian Glaciation

In comparison with previous periods, there is only sparse evidence from the Wolstonian Cold Stage (370,000–130,000 years ago) in Norfolk. An ice sheet covered the whole of west Norfolk for part of this phase. Some handaxes of this age have come from west Norfolk, in the vicinity of the fen edge, from South Wootton, Feltwell and Hockwold cum Wilton.

The Ipswichian Interglacial

The Ipswichian (last) Interglacial (130,000–115,000 years ago) left prolific evidence for its wildlife at gravel pits in the county's main river valleys. Summer temperatures were at least two degrees warmer than those of today.

The Devensian Glaciation

Between 115,000 and 11,500 years ago was the Devensian (last) Cold Stage. The period from about 20,000 to 15,000 BC saw the final advance of the ice sheets. This glaciation only just reached the now-coastal area of north-west Norfolk. Some sparse flora survived in unglaciated parts but there were no humans left anywhere in Britain at this time.

Then, the climate began to improve and our ancestors followed herds of game northwards and repopulated Britain as the land thawed. They crossed the area of land that joined Britain to Europe, and East Anglia became the main passageway. Genetic studies show very early cultural links between the peoples of Frisia, the North Sea Plain and Norfolk at this time.

It was during the Devensian period that modern humans first reached Britain. The 'moderns' are thought to have reached the British Isles about 33,000 years ago. Initially, they shared the landscape with Neanderthals, whom they eventually replaced. However, the Neanderthals also managed to leave a significant mark in Norfolk's archaeological record.

The final effects of the ice, at the end of the Devensian Cold Stage, were coming to an end about 11,500 BC. The climate and environment of Britain had begun to change. As conditions became milder, populations moved north into the area of Norfolk in increasing numbers, following herds of game. These people were presented with new opportunities for subsistence as they adapted to new, post-glacial conditions. The period following the final retreat of the glacial ice is known as the Mesolithic.

THE DRAINAGE OF NORFOLK

The drainage system of major rivers across East Anglia was originally very different to what we have today. The landscape was to develop and change significantly over a period of half a million years. During the Cromerian Warm Stage, the wider landscape embraced major river systems, which drained the mainland of Europe and flowed into the North Sea, which lay far to the north of its present position.

An ancestral River Thames flowed from south-west to north-east across the area of Essex, Suffolk and Norfolk. It was joined near Bury St Edmunds by another river flowing eastwards from the Midlands, north of modern Leicester, which we call the Bytham River. This flowed across Norfolk's fenland, which did not exist at that time. It entered Norfolk in the vicinity of King's Lynn and flowed eastwards, eventually through Lowestoft.

The subsequent onset of the Anglian Cold Stage destroyed the Bytham River. It also forced the ancestral River Thames further south to its present location.

After the Ice Age, the ice melted and the sea level rose, steadily encroaching upon the land. However, it was not until about 8,000 years ago that the coastline reached approximately its present-day position. From about 3,000 years ago until about 1,600 years ago, sea levels rose once again and coastal estuaries and marshes were extensively flooded. Today's rivers were broader and deeper and formed more formidable boundaries.

Today, rivers permeate the whole Norfolk landscape. The watershed runs in an arc through the clay land of central Norfolk and divides the rivers that flow towards the east coast from those that flow westward to the Wash.

Until about just 8,500 years ago, Britain remained joined to the continental mainland. Its swathes of temperate forest stretched all the way to the European mainland across what is now the North Sea.

NORFOLK'S ICE AGE LEGACY

The legacy of the Ice Age in East Anglia is the gentle landscape that we see today, which is the newest and flattest part of the British Isles in terms of its geology. Norfolk's rock formations are low lying and the lack of high hills and mountains has led people to remark on the 'big skies' that characterise the county and which have been depicted in the works of many artists, including those of the Norwich School, who were famously active in the early nineteenth century.

This part of Britain is acknowledged to contain the most comprehensive evidence for the Pleistocene Epoch and the Ice Age, which cover the period that we have designated as Deep History, when the first people inhabited Britain. In relation to archaeological terminology, this embraces the period known as the Palaeolithic.

The geological profile of the Pleistocene has been evidenced through the study of sections of Norfolk's coastal cliffs and from examining pits and borings further inland. It is through the study of these same fragile rocks and deposits that we can also trace an outline of our earliest prehistory. They contain strata that we are able to date and are rich in the bones and teeth of creatures and fragments of flora that once inhabited the area.

Although England's easternmost county contains what is the lowest high point in the country, the term 'flat' cannot be applied to the county as a whole. Much of the coastal area in the north and north-east contains cliffs and hills. Here are some of the most dramatic, undulating and varied natural features to be found throughout the region of East Anglia.

At the same time, this is a place where we can experience a sense of fragility of the landscape and engage with the concept of geological and climatic change, which has such a resonance for Britain in the twenty-first century. A visit to Norfolk's coast enables us to forge a profound connection between past millennia and the modern day.

EROSION AND DEPOSITION

Today, much of Norfolk's coast is subject to collapsing cliffs and shifting sands. The coastline is at a point of tension between erosion and sedimentation, echoing our theme of fragility. This dynamic coastline has been described as the most vulnerable corner of the British Isles.

The relatively young formations that comprise Norfolk's geology are poorly consolidated and they are not resilient to withstanding the forces of erosion. Delicate cliffs formed from glacial sands and gravels crumble away on a daily basis. Where they are exposed, the violent forces of nature are able to rapidly erode them.

Wind and waves wash away many tonnes of cliff material during storm conditions, while currents undercut the cliffs and cause further subsidence in many places.

Erosion is prominent on much of the east coast but sediments are also continuing to be laid down, especially in the estuaries, salt marshes and freshwater locations. Here, among the mudflats, lay the remains of molluscs and crustaceans, which will eventually become the fossils discovered by future generations.

Existing between these extremes presents a sense of uncertainty, especially for the population living in some of the more vulnerable stretches of the coastline. For decades, there have been efforts to protect the coast from destructive natural forces, through the construction of sea defences. Such human-made barriers have diverted waves but often inadvertently caused erosion on other parts of the coastline. The natural balance is one that we do not fully understand and any human intervention can readily tip these processes towards unforeseen outcomes, sometimes with disastrous consequences.

The natural balance is a delicate one. The area has been subjected to flooding for centuries and there have been dreadful occurrences within living memory.

On 31 January and 1 February 1953, 100 people were killed on Norfolk's east coast when a high spring tide and windstorm combined to produce an abnormal and lethal storm tide. Most recently, in 2018, the region experienced a different form of extreme destructive weather conditions; this time, with snow and low temperatures, dubbed 'The Beast from the East'. With the continuing melting of Arctic sea ice, we live in anticipation of the impact of more 'Beasts' in the years to come.

We have seen how Norfolk's natural setting has been forged by extreme climatic conditions, and life on this exposed part of the British coastline continues to be affected and disrupted by natural forces. In the next chapter, we shall look more closely at the formation of the land beneath our feet, which provides us with so much of the information from which we can reconstruct distant past times.

3. THE GEOLOGY

STRATIGRAPHY

The rocks directly beneath our feet tell the story of the world, millions of years deep into the past. At any moment, we may be standing on ground that was once a submerged seabed or perhaps a desert. Each section of sediment contains clues to how the world looked at a given time, long ago. It provides the story of an ever-changing landscape: from warm seas to frozen tundra and arid deserts to temperate river estuaries.

The concept of stratigraphy underpins our geological and archaeological interpretation and is a key method that is used in both disciplines. It is essentially the study of layering and deposition and is based on the principle of successive layers building up over time. Stratigraphy provides contexts for archaeological finds and is the basis of dating material in the ground.

If you were to drill a hole straight downwards, perhaps beneath a typical Norfolk seaside town like Cromer or Sheringham, in general, the deeper you go, the older the rocks get. As well as seeing sediments of different ages, you find that they are of very different types – each reflecting the environment in which they were originally formed. They exhibit some great contrasts and also reveal some surprises. For example, over millions of years, this landscape has witnessed desert, as well as ice, and has been covered by seas and cut by ancient rivers.

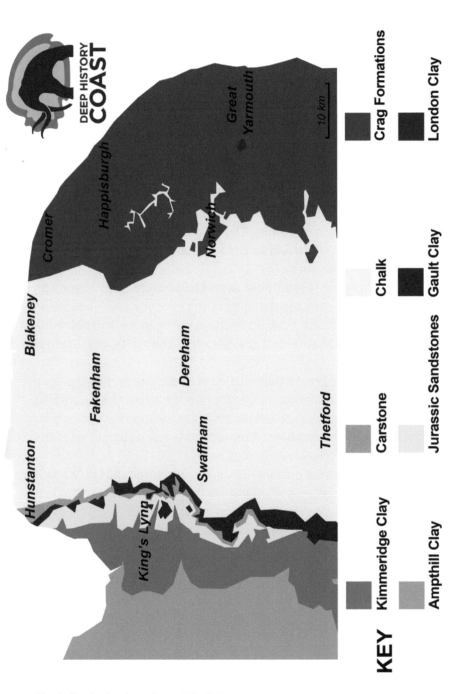

Fig. 8: The bedrock geology of Norfolk.

THE GEOLOGY OF THE DEEP HISTORY COAST

In most simple terms, Norfolk's geology can be separated into two principal layers. There are the underlying bedrock deposits, which slope gently eastwards, then above these are the superficial 'drift' deposits.

To the west lie the oldest sediments in the county, where the Jurassic mudstones and limestones of the Kimmeridge and Ampthill Clay Formations, to the west of King's Lynn and Downham Market, yield fossils of marine reptiles, such as plesiosaur and ichthyosaur bones. Just to the east of these are the early Cretaceous rocks. The Lower Cretaceous here includes the characteristic brown sandstone that is used in buildings in the far west of the county.

Further east is the Upper Cretaceous white chalk. Overlying the chalk are the Crag deposits of the Pliocene and Pleistocene periods. These are covered by the superficial ice-age deposits, which include tills and gravels, together with the Cromer Forest-Bed.

The different rocks that you find beneath your feet on the Deep History Coast provide an insight into the geodiversity present along the coast that, in turn, provides many different habitats for a diverse fauna and flora. A representative selection of what lies below us in Norfolk is described here.

The samples are presented in order of their age and tell us about the environment at specific times in the past. The three oldest samples come from a single borehole drilled at Gimingham, north of Mundesley, where the geologists were looking for coal. When none was found, they stopped drilling, which was at a substantial depth of 1,270m.

Contorted Boulder Clay
Briton's Lane Formation, Quaternary Period
Found: East Runton
Depth: 10m
Age: 0.4 million years
Environment: Ice Age glaciation

Shelly Gravel
Wroxham Crag Formation, Quaternary Period
Found: East Runton
Depth: 20m
Age: 1 million years
Environment: Temperate rivers, lakes and cool shallow seas

Chalk
Upper Chalk Formation, Cretaceous Period
Found: Beeston Regis
Depth: 35m
Age: 80 million years
Environment: Clear, warm sea

Siltstone with Ripple Marks
Mercia Mudstone Group, Triassic Period
Found: Gimingham Borehole
Depth: 1,080m
Age: 180 million years
Environment: Temporary desert lake

Coarse, Pebbly Sandstone
Sherwood Sandstone Group, Permian/Triassic Period
Found: Gimingham Borehole
Depth: 1,150m
Age: 225 million years
Environment: Desert alluvial fan, wadi bed

Limestone
Carboniferous Limestone Supergroup, Carboniferous Period
Found: Gimingham Borehole
Depth: 1,270m
Age: 325 million years
Environment: Tropical reef lagoon

We shall now look in more detail at the major geological deposits encountered on the Norfolk coast.

THE CRETACEOUS DEPOSITS

The oldest rocks to be found in north Norfolk were created during the Cretaceous period, a geological period that lasted from about 145 million to about 66 million years ago. In the west, the (older) Lower Cretaceous formations are characterised by the brown sandstone called Carstone. Those of the Upper Cretaceous, further east, are known as the White Chalk deposits, and within them are preserved the remains of a fascinating variety of ancient animals.

During the early Cretaceous period, between about 145 and 97 million years ago, there was an increase in sea level and the land surface was flooded. East Anglia and much of Europe were covered in a warm, wide sea. The climate was subtropical, and reptiles ruled the world. Dinosaurs dominated the land, while pterosaurs inhabited the skies. Giant marine reptiles such as ichthyosaurs, pliosaurs, mosasaurs and plesiosaurs (only distantly related to the dinosaurs) occupied the top of the food chain in the seas. They preyed upon sharks and other fish, turtles and crocodiles. These, in turn, fed upon animals such as smaller fish, ammonites and belemnites (extinct swimming molluscs related to today's cuttlefish).

On the seabed lived large numbers of sponges, corals, lobsters, crabs, molluscs, brachiopods, echinoids (sea urchins) and crinoids. These last two are related to modern starfish. Starfish have five 'limbs', and sea urchins and crinoids have a similar 'fivefold' pattern.

It was the countless millions of tiny plankton skeletons called coccoliths that accumulated on the sea floor which created the deep chalk deposits upon which most of Norfolk rests today, and can be seen exposed in the cliffs of the Deep History Coast.

Fig. 9: Reconstruction of the Cretaceous seas of Norfolk some 80 million years ago, showing a mosasaur hunting belemnites over the chalky seabed. Mosasaur teeth have been found across Norfolk and belonged to giant marine reptiles probably more closely related to today's monitor lizards than to the dinosaurs that lived on land at the time.

Fig. 10: The most commonly found fossils within the Cretaceous chalk deposits of the Deep History Coast: 1a. Fossilised sea sponge (*Ventriculites* sp.); 1b. Reconstruction of *Ventriculites* in life, 2a. Fossilised belemnite guard; 2b. Reconstruction of a belemnite in life; 3a. Fossilised sea urchin (*Echinocorys scutata*); 3b. Reconstruction of *E. scutata* in life. (Illustrations by David Waterhouse)

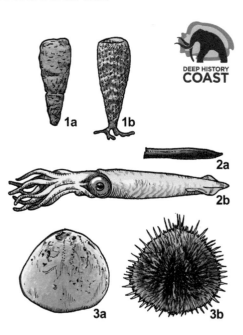

There were massive geological changes at the close of the Cretaceous period. The same earth movements that caused the formation of the Alps further south resulted in East Anglia being raised and the draining away of this Cretaceous sea (part of the extinct Tethys Ocean). From about 50 million years ago, East Anglia became dry.

THE CRAG DEPOSITS

The Cretaceous was followed by the Palaeogene period, which saw Norfolk become a land region once again. There was a gap of over 60 million years between the most recent chalk deposits and the creation of the next geological formation found on the Deep History Coast, which is known as the Crag. Sediments laid down during the intervening timespan were eroded away. No deposits from the Palaeocene to the Miocene Age (between about 66 and 5 million years ago) remain.

The Crag deposits were formed during the Pliocene, between about 5 and 2.6 million years ago, just before the last ice age, as conditions began to cool. The Crag formations cover much of East Anglia and their exact nature varies from place to place. Within these unexciting-looking sediments can be found the well-fossilised remains of sea-dwelling animals (such as molluscs, fish and occasionally dolphins, walrus and even whales) and also awe-inspiring, land-dwelling animals such as rhino, giant deer, wild horse and early species of mammoth. The fossils of land animals can be found among the sea creatures because their remains were occasionally carried out to sea by rivers.

The Crag Group is made up of layers of clays, muds, sands, gravels and pebbles. They are often cemented together by iron-rich sediments (which give the deposit a reddish or orange colour). They are generally between just over 2 and 5 million years old, and represent cool and temperate marine conditions, becoming gradually cooler as the ice ages approached.

The deepest and oldest of the Crag deposits is the Coralline Crag Formation, which consists of pale, sandy and marly beds with many fossils. It is found mostly in Suffolk.

Next oldest in age is the Red Crag Formation, which contains what's known as the 'Nodule Bed', found in Norfolk and Suffolk. This is followed by the Norwich Crag Formation and, finally, the uppermost (and therefore youngest deposit exposed in north Norfolk), the Wroxham Crag Formation.

THE WROXHAM CRAG

The Crag deposit you can see along the Deep History Coast at Weybourne is called the Wroxham Crag, which is a concreted, iron-rich sand, gravel and clay deposit, dating from about 3 to about 1.5 million years ago. It is found immediately above the chalk deposits.

It is formally known as the Weybourne Crag, as many of the best fossils have been found there. Its layers of clay, mud, sand, gravel and pebbles are often cemented together by iron-rich sediments. Within them lie fossil clams, oysters, sharks and other fish, whales, dolphins and an extinct type of walrus, as well as the occasional mammoth, bison and rhino.

THE ICE AGE DEPOSITS OF NORFOLK

The period following the Palaeogene is known as the Quaternary, which is the period of the Ice Age. Technically, we are still living in the Ice Age today, in an interglacial period called the Holocene, which began about 11,700 years ago.

Over the last 2.6 million years, the British Isles and the rest of Europe have experienced repeated cycles of warm and very cold climates associated with the Ice Age, as described in the previous chapter. Substantial quantities of sediments have been laid down during this time. These deposits provide information that shows a wide range of environmental conditions. They also provide evidence for a corresponding range of animal species that have, at different times, been native to the area. These will be considered in the next chapter.

Sediments found in Norfolk's cliffs, which include sands, clays and rocks, are known as till and were deposited by glacial action. They were transported and deposited by the ice, while other characteristic glacial features still visible in the modern landscape were also created.

THE FOREST-BED DEPOSITS

The Cromer Forest-Bed Formation, found on the Deep History Coast, contains river and woodland deposits that are about 500,000 to perhaps over 1 million years old. It is the richest source of fossils anywhere in the British Isles from the Pleistocene Epoch. Exposures of this formation can be found in cliffs from Weybourne in the north and as far south as Kessingland in Suffolk.

These important deposits have been studied for over 250 years and are vital to our understanding of how climate change affects animal populations. The Forest-Bed at West Runton is the Type Locality for the Cromerian Stage and is the benchmark against which all other sites of this age in Europe are measured.

The West Runton mammoth, which is the largest and oldest type of elephant ever found in the UK and probably the best example of its species in the world, was found in the Forest-Bed (see Chapter 6). This formation provides evidence for what was once a slow-moving river in a flat landscape that was rich in grassland, woodland plants and animals, much like the Norfolk Broads today. The climate of the time was almost identical to ours today.

SOME OTHER GEOLOGICAL FEATURES TO LOOK OUT FOR

Ironstones
Iron is a naturally occurring element and is found in many different rock types. Iron oxides are often found, giving them a characteristic red/brown, rusty colour. Ironstone nodules (or just ironstones) are sedimentary rocks that are usually a mixture of iron oxide and clay. They are often spherical, conical or rounded in shape as they generally formed around a central nucleus of a small fossil or piece of gravel. In Norfolk, many of the ironstones come from the Wroxham Crag.

Ironstones sometimes have a mud-crack pattern on their surface. This occurred when water evaporated from the sediment surface (a similar pattern occurs when muddy puddles dry out).

Ironstones can become highly polished by being washed around on the beach. The work of sculptors Henry Moore and Barbara Hepworth was influenced by the ironstone nodules they found on the beaches of Norfolk, in the vicinity of Happisburgh.

Ironstones can often be confused with other iron-rich materials. Iron meteorites are extremely rare and have a thin, black 'fusion crust', which forms when superheated during atmospheric entry. Ironstones do not have this characteristic fusion crust. Human-made iron slag can also be confused with natural ironstone. Iron slag is a mixture of iron oxides (but does not contain any clay). Iron slag often has a lava-like appearance, which natural sedimentary ironstones do not have.

Recycled Stones
Rivers carry pieces of broken and weathered rocks as they flow. When rivers reach lakes, or in this case, the sea, those rocks sink to the bottom. These build up over time in layers called sediments.

As more sediment builds up, it squashes the layers at the bottom, squeezing out water and allowing mineral crystals to form. The crystals act like cement and stick the sediment together. This is how the orange/brown layer (called the Crag) at the base of the cliffs at Weybourne formed, about 3 million years ago.

The flint pebbles that can be found on the beach at Weybourne formed within the chalk, in a tropical sea, about 80 million years ago. They eroded out of the chalk and have been slowly worn by the sea to form smooth, rounded stones. Eventually they will be weathered away to sand and the process of sedimentation will begin again.

OUR FOSSIL HERITAGE

The fossils that are found at locations on Norfolk's coast are important to science and education. They also form an extremely important part of our natural heritage. They are central to our understanding of how life has developed over millennia, as well as our knowledge of ancient environments.

Norfolk's Deep History Coast is one of the best places in the country to find fossils. They both connect us with our distant ancestors and form a link with the history of life on earth. These remains should be treated with the same consideration and care that we show to historical artefacts.

Fossil collecting is an enjoyable and rewarding experience, but only if it is carried out in a responsible manner will we be able to maintain our fossil heritage for future generations.

The art of finding fossils combines scientific skills with accumulated experience, together with a considerable amount of luck. Whether you are a research scientist, in school or a professional collector, it is important to remember that any fossil can provide us with a great deal of scientific information. It is therefore essential to collect fossils in a way that enables this information to be preserved for later use.

We will now describe some of the more common types that you might come across on the Deep History Coast.

Belemnites

These crayon-shaped fossils, which are commonly found in the Deep History Coast's chalk, are the remains of part of an extinct mollusc. More specifically, they are a sort of internal shell (called a guard or rostrum), similar to a cuttlefish bone. Mussels, scallops, snails, slugs, cuttlefish, octopuses, nautilus and extinct ammonites are all types of mollusc. The name 'belemnite' is derived from the Ancient Greek word for dart, referring to the pointed end of many belemnite guards.

There is evidence that belemnites first appeared in the late Triassic period (about 234 million years ago), but they became common in the Jurassic and Cretaceous periods (from 213 to 66 million years ago). They died out during the Cretaceous–Paleogene extinction event, about 66 million years ago (see Chapter 4).

In any single layer of the chalk, there is rarely more than a single species of belemnite present. This observation is very useful for correlating rocks of the same age. Belemnites lived in relatively shallow waters, close to the shore. Some rare fossils have shown that they possessed ink sacs, like modern squid and octopuses. Belemnite ecology closely resembled that of modern squid; they were predators, they grew extremely rapidly, they bred once, laid their eggs and then died. They were particularly common during the period when the Norfolk chalk was being deposited, about 78–73 million years ago. In just one very large quarry in south Norfolk (working on the basis that there were on average three belemnite guards per square metre), it is possible that an astonishing total of between 100,000 and 135,000 are present there.

Originally, the guard of the belemnite was made of alternating thin layers of calcite and organic material. Fossilisation recrystallised the guard so that it is denser and heavier than it was in life. Fossil belemnites consist of crystals of calcite radiating from the centre of the guard. If you look at a complete guard, you can see that there is a circular hole at one end. This is the entrance to a conical hole called the alveolus. There is also a narrow slit connecting the outside of the guard to the alveolus. This is the ventral fissure and indicates where the underside of the animal would have been. The phragmacone is the chambered, conical-shaped part of the shell. The external part of the phragmacone is quite fragile and is usually not found in fossils.

The purpose of the belemnite guard was to ensure that the belemnite's centre of gravity and centre of buoyancy were close to each other. This balanced them within the water. All cephalopods can manoeuvre by expelling a jet of water through a funnel in their body called the hyponome, but belemnites also had fins. Their streamlined, torpedo-shaped body meant that they could move very swiftly through the water, much like squid can today.

In order to identify species of belemnite accurately, the guard has to be measured carefully at several key points. Serious researchers may also split the fossil along its length to reveal further important anatomical features. However, in the chalk of east Norfolk, along the Deep History Coast, the main belemnite genera are *Gonoteuthis*, *Belemnitella* and *Belemnella*. Of these, *Belemnitella* is by far the most common.

Sea Urchins

Echinoids (sea urchins) are related to crinoids (sea lilies) and starfish. They all share a five-fold symmetry, which you can see most clearly in the five arms of a starfish. This group of animals is diverse and relatively common as fossils within the chalk. The echinoids are the most widely encountered of these animals, in particular, *Echinocorys*, *Conulus* and *Micraster*.

Most of the echinoids found in the Deep History Coast chalk lived on the surface of the sea floor, but a few were shallow burrowers. The 'tests' (shells) of these fossil echinoids are often found complete, but it is much rarer to find their spines still attached.

Like starfish, echinoids have a skeleton composed of calcitic plates embedded in their skin. These plates form the test of a sea urchin. Regular echinoids have perfect five-fold symmetry, but irregular echinoids are also bilaterally symmetrical, which often makes them heart-shaped.

Just like starfish, echinoids have what are termed 'tube feet'. They move using these feet as well as their spines. The tube feet extended out of small pores (which you can still see in many of their fossils). Each spine is attached to a circular 'tubercle' on the surface of the test.

Echinoids can be preserved in a number of different ways:

- Their calcitic plates may be intact, but flint or chalk has filled the inside.
- The plates may have disappeared, leaving an impression of the inside cast in flint.
- An impression of the plates may be left in a piece of flint. This is an external mould.

The fossil echinoid species that you are most likely to come across on the Deep History Coast is called *Echinocorys scutata*. This comes in a wide variety of shapes and sizes, which is extremely useful as the different varieties are from different layers within the chalk, helping geologists to identify how old each layer is.

Sponges

Sponges are also known as Poriferans, from the Latin words *porus*, 'pore', and *ferre*, 'to bear'. Believe it or not, they are actually primitive animals, and are mostly stationary water-dwellers that pump water through their porous skeletons to filter out food particles.

Sponges are among the simplest of animals. They don't have muscles, nerves or internal organs. In some ways, they are closer to being colonies of individual cells than multicellular organisms. There are over 5,000 known modern species of sponge, although species new to science are being discovered regularly.

The structure of sponges is simple. They are shaped like tubes, with one end stuck to a rock or other object. The open end is called the osculum, and the interior is the 'spongocoel'. The walls contain tiny pores that allow water to flow through the spongocoel.

It is thought that the earliest multicelled life on earth was a sponge-like creature. Certainly, the earliest known multicelled animal fossils are sponges from China that are roughly 600 million years old.

Sponges have not been studied as extensively as some other groups of animals, and there may be some surprises still left to be found about them. For example, it has recently been shown that some sponges are not stationary and can move to more favourable locations as rapidly as a few centimetres a day.

Modern sponges are mostly marine, ranging from the intertidal zone to depths in excess of 8,500m. A few species have adapted to freshwater environments. They are worldwide in their distribution and range from polar waters to the tropics. However, they are most abundant (both as individuals and numbers of species) in warmer waters.

Adult sponges remain attached to surfaces (such as rocky seabeds) and mostly remain stationary. Some are able to attach themselves to soft sediment by means of a root-like base. Because their pores are easily blocked by sediment, they tend to live in quiet, clear waters.

Commonly, the term sponge is applied to just the skeletons of these creatures. Commercial sponges are derived from various species and come in a variety of grades, from fine soft 'lamb's wool' type, to the coarse grades used for washing cars. Marine sponges come from fisheries in the Mediterranean and West Indies. The manufacture of rubber, plastic and cellulose-based synthetic sponges has significantly reduced the commercial sponge-fishing industry over recent years. (Loofahs, which are often confused with sponges, are actually the dried fruit of plants of the genus *Luffa*.)

The fossil record of sponges dates back to the Precambrian (600 million years ago). Some fossil sponges have worldwide distribution, while others are restricted to certain areas.

In Europe, the Jurassic limestone of the Swabian Alps is composed largely of sponge remains, some of which are well preserved. Many sponges are found in the Cretaceous Lower

Greensand and chalk formations of England, and in rocks from the upper part of the Cretaceous period in France. A famous locality for fossil sponges is the Cretaceous Faringdon Sponge Gravels in Oxfordshire.

Although sponges are common fossils within the chalk of the Deep History Coast, they remain little studied (major reference works date from the 1840s, 1880s, 1950s and 1960s). Part of the reason they are so difficult to study is because of the complicated processes needed to distinguish between different species. This involves dissolving the fossils in acid and then thin-sectioning the tiny spicules (skeletal elements made of silica). However, with a little know-how, most fossil sponges can be identified to some degree.

Fossil sponges vary in size from 1cm to more than 1m. They also vary greatly in shape, from vase-shaped (such as *Ventriculites*), spherical (such as *Porosphaera*), pear-shaped (such as *Siphonia*) and branching (such as *Doryderma*).

Without sponges, we wouldn't have flint! The mineral silica (which is mainly what flint is made of) comes from the spicules of billions and billions of ancient sponges. Unusual chemistry in the ocean that covered East Anglia about 70–90 million years ago, led to the silica from sponges being dissolved in seawater. This silica then solidified out of the water to form flint. The spherical 'cannon-shot' flints that can be found across Norfolk are naturally formed, having been weathered and rolled in water. However, many of these flints were vaguely spherical to start with, as they formed around sponges such as *Porosphaera*.

EARLY FOSSIL COLLECTORS

The serious and systematic collection and identification of fossils began in the nineteenth century through the work of dedicated amateurs. Even today, many important discoveries, such as the West Runton mammoth, are made by members of the public. There were some highly renowned early collectors in Norfolk.

Anna Gurney (1795–1857) was a scholar, geologist and philanthropist. As a child, she contracted polio, which paralysed her lower limbs, meaning that from a young age she was a wheelchair user. The Gurney family were influential Quakers, who played a major part in the redevelopment of Norwich. They also established Gurney's Bank in 1770, which merged into Barclays Bank in 1896. All of this meant that they were a wealthy family, with advantages that a lot of disabled people living in the eighteenth and nineteenth centuries did not have access to.

Anna focused her geological research on local portions of the Cromer Forest-Bed Formation. According to the *Bury and Norwich Post*, dated 14 December 1821, she presented to the Geological Society, 'various bones of the fossil elephant, found on the coast of Norfolk between Cromer and Happisburgh'. Later, in 1845, she became the first ever female member of the British Archaeological Association.

After her death, she donated the majority of her extensive fossil collection to the Norfolk and Norwich Museum (now Norwich Castle Museum and Art Gallery), including important fossils such as woolly mammoth, hippopotamus, Deninger's bear (an early form of brown bear) and steppe mammoth.

John Gunn (1801–90) was the Rector of Irstead and Barton Turf (near Stalham, north Norfolk). Gunn had a lifelong love of geology. He said that it was the discovery of the fossil remains of hippos and elephants in the cliffs at Happisburgh that fired his imagination. He asked his father how it was that such tropical animals could have lived in Norfolk in the past. His father replied, 'There is much to be done before that can be made out.' He dedicated a great deal of his life to looking for answers. Much of his collection is now held at Norwich Castle Museum.

Alfred Savin (1860–1948) was a Cromer man who ran a shop in Church Street. He wrote the *History of Cromer*, which remains an important reference book to this day. It is said he began collecting fossils at the age of 6. Much of his collection was acquired in his lifetime by the Natural History Museum, London, but many specimens are held at Cromer Museum and Norwich

Castle Museum. Many fossils bear his name, such as *Megaloceros savini* – an extinct species of giant deer. For nearly half a century, the little shop in Church Street, its window filled with elephant teeth, amber and silverware, was a rendezvous for geologists and palaeontologists from many countries.

These three remarkable people, together with many other collectors over the years, have shaped our understanding of the distant geological past. As you walk along Norfolk's Deep History Coast and learn about the worlds that once existed here, it is men and women such as Gurney, Gunn and Savin who we have to thank for revealing this exciting story.

REPORTING YOUR FOSSIL FINDS

If you are fortunate enough to make any unusual or rare finds, please do report them to any of Norfolk's museums listed in Chapter 9. NMS offers an identification service for those who discover fossils in the county. Once identified, specialists will return your finds, together with a full professional identification. Allowing staff to record the finds ensures that we can improve our understanding of Norfolk's past and recreate just what the area looked like and what lived there at different stages through time.

In this chapter, we have reviewed the geological background. In the following chapters, we shall trace the sites of the Deep History Coast and their archaeological significance. Before doing so, we shall first consider the changing fauna of the area.

4. THE CHANGING FAUNA

EXTINCTION EVENTS

We have seen in Chapter 2 how life on earth has had to contend with a range of natural forces, which gave rise to the conditions that eventually led to the evolution of humans. The effects of changes in the atmosphere and oceans, climate change and volcanic activity have also presented massive challenges for life on the planet through a series of great extinction events.

There have been five such extinctions of life on earth; all of which occurred many millions of years ago and long before humans appeared. Their causes are still not thoroughly understood but the first four appear to have been the result of planetary forces. These occurred:

- 440 million years ago – the Ordovician-Silurian transition extinction was caused by global warming and volcanism.
- 365 million years ago – the Late Devonian extinction.
- 252 million years ago – the Permian-Triassic extinction was the earth's largest extinction event.
- 201 million years ago – the Triassic-Jurassic transition extinction.
- 66 million years ago – the Cretaceous-Paleogene extinction was mainly caused by an asteroid impact and was responsible for the end of the dinosaurs.

It was in the aftermath of the last great extinction that conditions gave rise to the origin of the primates, beginning about 56 million years ago.

Humankind is currently accelerating the natural planetary processes and we are now in danger of presiding over a sixth catastrophic event, which is already being termed the 'Holocene extinction'. Today, as we write this book, there is an imminent threat of losing about 37,500 species, many of which we have shared our planet with for thousands of years.

In this chapter we shall concentrate on the changing fauna of Norfolk in relation to the period of Deep History, since the presence of humans in the area.

NORFOLK'S NATIVE FAUNA

It is not only the story of our human past that is being revealed along the Deep History Coast. Humans have not made their journey alone. We have interacted with other creatures at all stages. We have exploited, eaten and domesticated many of these species. The climatic and environmental changes related in Chapter 2 also influenced the natural fauna. Of course, the story of humankind developed hand in hand with that of other animals and plants. As the climate fluctuated with the ice age phases, a whole range of species moved north and south to avoid the most severe conditions.

Spectacular discoveries of creatures that have inhabited Norfolk over thousands of years continue to be made. Some of these species are familiar to us today, although many are no longer found in the British Isles.

Norfolk has seen exceptional diversity in the species that have lived here. As we have seen, most of its geology is relatively young, owing much to the Ice Age, and does not contain evidence for dinosaurs, who lived much earlier and on the land further west. But it was home to a wide range of other creatures, including giants that we term 'megafauna'. In fact, many of these huge animals were much larger than any dinosaurs that ever lived in Britain.

Norfolk's native fauna has also changed significantly over millennia, as the climate has fluctuated. There were extinctions of some species and migrations of others from different places. In fact, it is impossible to state exactly what should be considered to be the native fauna, as this would differ profoundly depending on the precise date in question over the last million years.

The area has seen a series of changing ecosystems over time. Through contact with the wider world, it has absorbed waves of immigrant species and been the home of many fascinating and diverse creatures. Both animals and plants have adapted to changing habitats.

Today, the British Isles are not rich in types of mammals, with just forty native terrestrial species listed. There was much greater diversity throughout the period of Deep History. In prehistoric times, some large and exotic beasts, which we call megafauna, were exploited by the inhabitants.

NORFOLK'S 'CHARISMATIC MEGAFAUNA'

In the past, the Deep History Coast would have been a much more dangerous place for a stroll. If you were there about 500,000 years ago, you might have come across prides of lions, packs of wolves and clans of spotted hyaenas. Several other large cats would have terrorised the local wildlife, including lynx, European jaguar and even a scimitar-tooth cat called *Homotherium*.

Enormous bears would have meandered across the plains. There were also smaller meat-eating animals such as stoats, weasels, pine martens and an extinct type of otter that would have munched on the smaller birds, mammals and fish of the area.

The vegetarians weren't much safer either. You would have needed to dodge grumpy steppe mammoths, short-tempered rhinos, rutting giant deer, belligerent bison and even mischievous macaque monkeys!

Of course, these striking species did not continue to inhabit Norfolk. Many died out; the changing climate being a significant factor. However, the role played by humans was perhaps the most significant. The expansion of people, who hunted selected species, opened up the landscape and introduced new species, possibly had the most profound impact.

Sadly, it was our ancestors who were largely responsible for killing off most of the larger land mammals. Humans played an especially significant role in the decline of the megafauna. The larger creatures, such as mammoths, had become extinct in the region by 12,000 years ago.

THE ICE AGE FAUNA

The ice age cycles had a profound effect on the animals and plants living here. During severely cold periods (which could last for tens of thousands of years), ice caps formed over the highlands of Europe and expanded, covering much of the land in sheets of ice, in places up to 4km thick.

When this happened, many animals retreated to southern Europe, where it was slightly warmer. Some species did not survive the harsh conditions and became extinct. Other animals, such as reindeer, bison, woolly mammoths and woolly rhinos, thrived as they were adapted to living in cool climates.

When conditions improved during the occasional warmer but shorter interglacial periods, the ice sheets melted and retreated north, leaving behind the debris they had brought with them on their journey. The cold-adapted animals would retreat northwards as well.

The British Isles were connected to Europe as a peninsula for much of this period, so each time the conditions improved, some animals were able to make their way back from their refuges in southern Europe. During the warmest phases, hyaenas, elephants, monkeys, pond terrapins and hippos lived in Norfolk.

Fossils of both warm-adapted and cold-adapted animals are found regularly on the Deep History Coast. In fact, the fossils and sediments preserved in Norfolk during the ice ages are the most significant in the British Isles for this time period and are among the very best in Europe. Every year, students come from far and wide to study them in order to learn about the interaction between climate and landscape.

The county's geology has revealed a wealth of evidence for the exotic species that once lived in the area. The Cromer Forest-Bed Formation, which was mentioned in the previous chapter, contains a deposit sometimes referred to as the Freshwater Bed. The exposure on the north Norfolk coast provides evidence for a rich and diverse fauna. Once again, an excursion through the Ice Age will illustrate the great diversity of creatures that have inhabited this area.

Following the Beestonian Glacial, during the Cromerian Interglacial there were regular mass migrations of herd animals. Evidence collected from the Freshwater Bed deposits shows that there were fauna that would be familiar to us today but also larger and more exotic species present. These included rhinoceros, elephant, wild boar, lion, spotted hyaena and macaque monkeys.

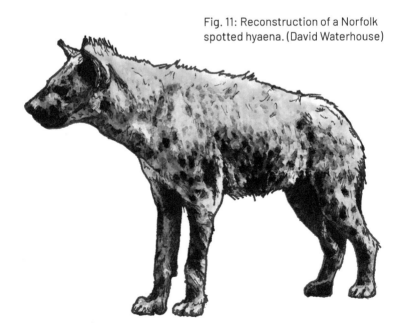

Fig. 11: Reconstruction of a Norfolk spotted hyaena. (David Waterhouse)

In the Anglian glaciation, there were some ice-free intervals during which the vegetation was mainly grasses and sedges. Gravel deposits beside the River Waveney, such as those at Homersfield (just over the border into Suffolk), provide rich evidence for the diverse megafauna of this time, with remains of woolly mammoth, woolly rhinoceros, reindeer and bison.

The Hoxnian Interglacial saw the reappearance of temperate vegetation and its associated animals. Temperate mammal fauna included beaver, horse, red and fallow deer, rhinoceros and, again, macaque monkeys.

Evidence for the Wolstonian glaciation is found in the River Waveney terrace gravels and the site of Broome Heath, which contain fossils of mammoth and bison.

The Ipswichian Interglacial is represented by finds from Swanton Morley, Shropham and Beetley. Fossils include those of large mammals such as hippopotamus, an extinct straight-tusked elephant and aurochs (the ancestor of most modern domesticated cattle). Pollen records indicate that the land was covered by temperate forest at that time.

In the Devensian glaciation, the climate began to improve and our ancient relatives followed herds of game northwards and repopulated Britain as the land thawed. Mammoths and woolly rhinos returned towards the end of the period but they became extinct everywhere in Europe by about 12,000 years ago.

At Shropham, in south-central Norfolk, abundant bones of bison and reindeer have been found, which show that vast herds crossed the ancestral River Thet on seasonal migrations. The concentration of bones is evidence for a high mortality at this crossing place. This scenario is reminiscent of the African Serengeti today, where predators congregate at river crossings to pick off migrating wildebeest.

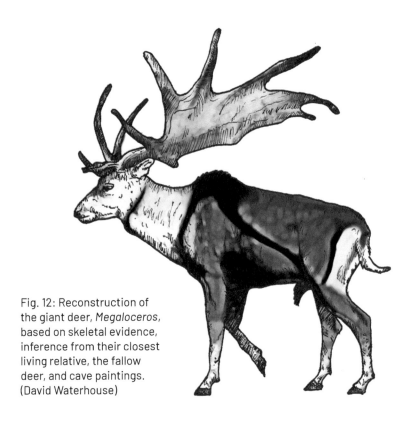

Fig. 12: Reconstruction of the giant deer, *Megaloceros*, based on skeletal evidence, inference from their closest living relative, the fallow deer, and cave paintings. (David Waterhouse)

DEER, OH DEER!

Today, six species of deer live wild in the UK. If you look hard enough, you can find them all somewhere in Norfolk. However, only red (*Cervus elaphus*) and roe deer (*Capreolus capreolus*) are considered native today – having made it here without the help of us humans.

Fallow deer (*Dama dama*) are generally considered an introduced animal, as the Normans brought them over in the eleventh century. However, they used to roam the UK before an especially cold period in the last ice age wiped them out, so perhaps we should think of them as being 'reintroduced'?

If you were on the Deep History Coast about 1 million years ago, you would have seen many more types of deer nibbling on the grass and munching on the leaves nearby. As well as familiar red, roe and fallow deer, there would have been giant deer (*Megaloceros* spp., *Euctenoceros* spp., *Libralces* spp.), Roberts fallow deer (*Dama roberti*) and the unbelievable-looking broad-fronted moose (*Cervalces latifrons*).

MAMMOTHS

Skip-loads of mammoth bones have been dredged up from the bed of the North Sea by trawlers operating from both the Netherlands and England. These ancient survivals continue to show that the area now covered by deep water and once connected to Britain was once home to large groups of these huge mammals.

The three species of elephant alive today (the African bush, African forest and the Asian elephant) are all that remain of a very diverse group of elephantids. Elephants evolved and diversified during the last 5 million years. The earliest species lived in the tropical woodlands of Africa, but later species migrated into Europe, Asia and even North America.

Elephant fossils (which include the mammoths) are relatively common on the Deep History Coast. Mastodon, such as *Anancus arvernensis*, have been discovered in the Pliocene and Pleistocene deposits of Norfolk (about 5 to 2 million years ago). Gigantic straight-tusked elephants (*Palaeoloxodon antiquus*) were found here during warm conditions of the interglacial periods of the Middle and Late Pleistocene (from about 780,000 years ago).

However, it is for mammoths that the Deep History Coast is particularly famous. These were a group of elephants that specialised in eating grasses and shrubs of the cooler areas of northern Europe. When the Ice Age brought freezing temperatures to most of the continent, mammoths were well adapted to survive. Norfolk, and especially the Deep History Coast, is one of the best places in the world to find mammoth fossils because its geology contains sediments of the right age (from the last 3 million years).

Mammuthus meridionalis, the southern mammoth, is the ancestor of the two later species found on the Deep History Coast. It lived between about 3 million and 750,000 years ago in Europe. Its diet was varied, consisting of grasses, shrubs and trees.

Mammuthus trogontherii, the steppe mammoth, replaced its ancestor species, the southern mammoth, about 750,000 years ago. However, because some southern mammoths migrated into Asia, the two species actually co-existed for a while in what is now the Deep History Coast, and contemporary deposits in locations such as Happisburgh, from 800,000 to nearly 1 million years ago, actually contain both species for a period of time.

The large steppe mammoths ate grasses, but also trees and shrubs. It was probably the largest species of elephant ever to have lived. It weighed at least 10 tonnes and stood 4m high at the shoulder. The famous West Runton mammoth skeleton (see Chapter 6) is from this species. The largest living elephants today weigh only about 5 tonnes and are 3–3.5m high.

Fig. 13: Reconstruction of the West Runton mammoth. (David Waterhouse)

One group of *Mammuthus trogontherii* evolved into *Mammuthus primigenius*, the woolly mammoth, during intensely cold periods of the ice ages about 500,000 to 300,000 years ago. Woolly mammoths were able to survive in cold environments, not just because of their woolly coats, but because they adapted to survive on a grass-rich diet. This was essential because during cold periods only grasses, sedges, mosses and certain wild flowers could survive in northern Europe.

The fossils of mammoths are among the most commonly found vertebrate remains along the Deep History Coast. However, most of these are fragments of the bones, tusks and teeth of these huge creatures.

By far the easiest way to tell the fossils of the three different Deep History Coast mammoths apart is by looking at their teeth. Like elephants today, mammoths had large tusks, which were modified incisor teeth, but they had only four molars in use at any one time.

Each type of mammoth had a slightly different type of molar, adapted for eating slightly different food. Southern mammoths required fewer enamel plates (lamellae) because they ate soft leaves, which were easily chewed. Woolly mammoths, however, ate tough sedges and grasses, so they needed a greater number of plates in order to grind their food.

As the different species evolved, the enamel plates that made up the teeth became more numerous, but the enamel thickness decreased over time. If you find a whole mammoth molar on the Deep History Coast, made up of lots of plates (eighteen or more), it is most likely to be from a woolly mammoth. If there are slightly fewer plates (perhaps fifteen), it is probably from their ancestor, the steppe mammoth. But, if there are only eight or nine plates, it is probably a southern mammoth molar.

It was between about 40,000 and 10,000 years ago that many of the large mammals became extinct in Europe. Mammoths died out just 12,000 years ago, with the exception of two small populations. One of those survived on St Paul Island, west of Alaska, until about 6,000 years ago, and another located on Wrangel Island in the

Arctic Ocean, north of Siberia, lasted until about 4,000 years ago. That means that there were still woolly mammoths on the planet when the Pyramids at Giza were being built! Their extinction was probably due to a combination of global climatic changes, together with the more successful hunting techniques of modern humans.

THE 'VOLE CLOCK'

Establishing a chronological framework is key to our understanding of the past. Applying appropriate methods of dating our very early archaeology and fossil sites is extremely important in order to enable us to build up a picture of how and when developments and changes occurred. There are a number of different dating methods available, although each has its limitations.

Most people have heard of radiocarbon dating. Unfortunately, most of the Deep History Coast is just too old for this technique to be applied. It is only reliable as far back as about 50,000 years ago. Alternatively, the Potassium-Argon method can date volcanic rocks back over millions of years but it is not appropriate for the geology of the Deep History Coast.

A reliable method of establishing chronology can involve the presence or absence of particular biological species. We can also trace dateable evolutionary changes in mammals during the Pleistocene.

Believe it or not, the most useful example in relation to our coastline is the humble water vole. Study of its evolution has enabled us to detect a significant development involving changes in its dentition. There was a development from rooted, in *Mimomys pusillus*, to unrooted incisors, in *Arvicola cantiana*, which occurred between 700,000 and 600,000 years ago. The presence of *Mimomys* and absence of *Arvicola* at a site can thus confirm the antiquity of a specific geological deposit or vice versa. This change in their anatomy has provided a dating horizon of significance in relation to the human story and the periods when different species of hominin were present.

MINI-BEASTS, BIG ANSWERS

It is possible for us to reconstruct past environments by studying the remains of creatures found during excavations, which come from firm contexts. The surviving parts of different mammals, including their bones, teeth and antlers, can provide some idea of past habitats, such as whether the location had been woodland, open grassland or wetland. However, one of the best environmental indicators is invertebrates.

Although their recovery is a painstaking process, the remains of insects can provide some of the best environmental evidence. Because each type of insect can only live within a narrow range of temperatures and environments, they can tell us an amazing amount about past climatic and environmental conditions on archaeological sites.

The remains of insects found during excavations on the Deep History Coast have been studied and now enable us to understand the landscape and climate at intervals in the past, such as where the West Runton mammoth lived. Research is continuing to provide us with valuable evidence in the interpretation and recreation of what conditions were like throughout the Ice Age.

POST-GLACIAL NORFOLK

The species present on the Deep History Coast from about 12,000 years ago are revealed to us by the diet of the resident hunter-gatherer population, during the period known as the Mesolithic (Middle Stone Age). Archaeologists have found evidence in the form of animal bones and shells from sites where they lived. These hunter-gatherers were drawn to Norfolk's coast and river systems, where they were able to exploit sea fish, sea mammals and marine shellfish.

The resources provided by wet landscapes similar to that of the broadland and fens were of sufficient importance to attract people from a considerable distance for specialised or seasonal exploitation, notably for the abundant fish, waterfowl and shellfish. Fish were caught with barbed hooks made from slivers of antler. Red and roe deer and wild pig bones are prominent on these sites. People also hunted aurochs and European elk.

The domestic dog (*Canis lupus familiaris*) was also present in Britain from at least as early as Mesolithic times. This was before the introduction of agriculture and the arrival of other domestic species.

The following archaeological period, called the Neolithic (New Stone Age), is associated with the introduction of farming. Neolithic settlements are found in East Anglia from about 4300 BC. Four species of domestic livestock were initially introduced – sheep, goats, cattle and pigs.

Sheep (*Ovis aries*) and goats (*Capra hircus*) were originally natives of the Middle East and had no wild ancestors in Britain. Cattle and pigs did both have wild ancestors, which were aurochs (*Bos primigenius*) and wild boar (*Sus scrofa*). The domestication of these animals enabled settlements to become more permanent and there was subsequently less need for people to move around the countryside. From this time on, the population began to increase, as a result of the new lifestyle.

The final stage of the prehistoric period was the Iron Age, which can be dated in Britain from about 700 BC. By this time, most of the larger and fiercer creatures had become extinct or moved away from lowland Britain. The full range of domesticated animals continued to be exploited on the farmsteads that covered the landscape.

We also have the emergence of a new form of evidence for the animal species, in the form of Celtic art, from which we gain an additional insight into the creatures at this time. A range of objects of the period depict the animals that were present, both on farms and in wilder parts of the landscape.

Species depicted in Norfolk include the boar, bull, duck, swan, horse and wolf, although it is thought that wolves were no longer present in Norfolk at that time. The animals were represented as figurines, decorative fittings attached to drinking vessels, cosmetic items and on the earliest coinage; their images permeating different aspects of everyday life.

The inspiration for zoomorphic objects during the Iron Age was often associated with religion and myth. We know that animals were venerated and sacrificed in rituals and their remains revered. Parts of their carcasses were mysteriously left unconsumed inside pits and features within settlements and houses. Some animals were even thought to possess magical powers.

MODERN THREATS

Today, Norfolk's diverse coastline and varied geology provide a wealth of habitats for wildlife. They offer a mixture of wetlands, sandbanks, shingle beaches, sand dunes, cliffs, salt marshes, mudflats and even a coastal chalk 'reef'. The winter storms, tidal fluctuations and occasional floods make this a shifting and changing coast, containing a range of specialised locations for fauna, maritime and botanical specimens.

One of the attractions of Norfolk in the twenty-first century is its comparatively undeveloped landscape. Enthusiasts come to watch a great diversity of birds and other wildlife.

The television programmes *Springwatch* and *Autumnwatch* are regular visitors, basing their programmes from locations on and around the coast.

Wild Ken Hill, at Snettisham, has become a favoured location for the series. A project is under way there, located at a farm adjacent to the Wash. Its aims are to combine the principles of rewilding, featuring species including beaver, with regenerative agriculture. Pensthorpe Nature Reserve lies further inland, next to Fakenham. It too has welcomed the BBC team. It contains a rich range of habitats, including wetlands, breck, heath and farmland.

But as urban development of the county encroaches on natural habitats, even Norfolk's wildlife is coming under threat. Species of birds, mammals and insects are undergoing significant falls in their numbers. In particular, fish and other marine life, including lobsters and crabs, are in serious decline. The maritime habitat provided by Cromer's unique, so-called chalk reef is also delicately poised. We shall return to that particular feature in Chapter 6.

Some recent developments are providing a more positive outlook. Species such as seals and otters have seen a revival in recent years and the reintroduction of regionally extinct species has also been started in appropriate places. In 2022, Britain's largest bird of prey, the sea eagle (or white-tailed eagle), was being reintroduced to west Norfolk after a century's absence, in addition to the beavers at Snettisham and Sculthorpe Moor.

The warming of summer temperatures is providing conditions for some exotic creatures to exploit. In 2022, bee-eaters, a migratory species of brightly coloured birds of southern Europe and Africa, have been found nesting at Trimingham, immediately inland from the north-east coast.

Having now reviewed the spectacular and diverse fauna that has inhabited the Deep History Coast, we can take a closer look at the arrival of another species – our own relatives, the first humans.

5. THE FIRST HUMANS

THE EARLIEST PEOPLE

The first people to arrive on the Deep History Coast can currently be traced back to nearly 1 million years ago. Bones of early humans are extremely rare in Britain and none have yet been found in Norfolk. The evidence that we do encounter is mainly in the form of their flint tools, which can sometimes indicate their sites of occupation.

In order to understand who these earliest inhabitants were, we need to introduce them by way of looking at the origins of the human family. We shall initially consider when the very first humans appeared and where they came from.

The Origins of Humans

As has been discussed in Chapter 2, we know that humans originated in Africa, where geology and climate had combined in a unique way that provided the optimum environmental conditions. All of the major subsequent developments in the process of human evolution similarly occurred in East Africa.

Humans are part of the larger family of primates, known as hominids, which includes the great apes. We separated from our closest living relatives, the chimpanzees, between 6–8 million years ago. Our own genus is defined by the name *Homo*, which distinguishes us from the other primates. The term 'hominin' refers to all modern and extinct human species, excluding the great apes. We are now the only surviving species of hominin, although there have been others, who we shall consider throughout this chapter.

The first hominin for which we have good fossil remains is *Ardipithecus ramidus*, who lived about 4.4 million years ago. By 4 million years ago, the hominins known as *Australopithecus* were able to walk upright. They are known to us through the well-preserved skeleton of a young female, who has been given the name Lucy, and who died by a stream in what is now Ethiopia, where her body was buried naturally and preserved. Lucy stood to a height of just 1.1m (3ft 7in).

Our own genus, *Homo*, emerged from *Australopithecus*, in the form of *Homo habilis*, evolving in Africa over 2 million years ago with a bodily form similar to our own. Their lifestyle was that of hunter-gatherers.

The most long-lasting species of *Homo* is *Homo erectus*, who first appeared about 2 million years ago. Their anatomy was similar to that of modern humans. Until that point, all hominins had only lived in Africa.

Homo erectus started to move out of Africa about 1.8 million years ago. In Europe, they evolved into the Neanderthals (*H. neanderthalensis*).

The *Homo erectus* population that remained in Africa produced modern humans (*H. sapiens*) between 300,000 and 200,000 years ago. Our species first dispersed out of Africa between about 100,000 and 55,000 years ago. On the way through Europe and Asia, we encountered and interacted with descendants of previous waves of hominins in the form of Neanderthals and Denisovans (*H. denisova*), the latter of which inhabited Asia.

BRITAIN'S DEEP HISTORY

The period from the very first presence of humans until approximately 10,000 BC is referred to by the archaeological term Palaeolithic (Old Stone Age), during which time the evolution of different human species occurred. As far as we know, four different species of human have lived in the British Isles, and Norfolk is currently the only county to have evidence of all four of these.

The Palaeolithic has been separated into three phases, which are called Lower, Middle and Upper. The Lower coincides approximately with the time of the earliest humans to move out of Africa and into Europe. The Upper Palaeolithic in Europe begins with the appearance of the first *Homo sapiens*, or anatomically modern humans.

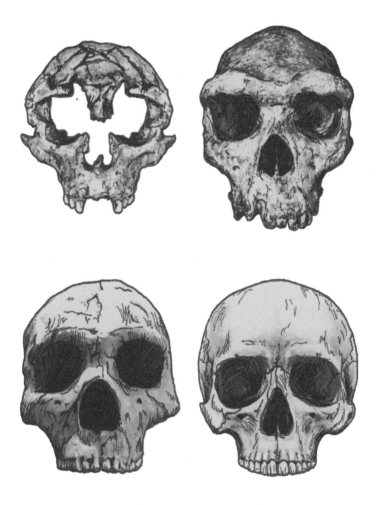

Fig. 14: Early hominin skulls (clockwise from top left): *Homo antecessor* ('Pioneer man'), *Homo heidelbergensis* ('Heidelberg man'), *Homo sapiens* (modern human), *Homo neanderthalensis* (Neanderthal). (David Waterhouse)

It is seldom appreciated that the human occupation of this country was not a single, continuous process. In fact, archaeology can trace a series of separate occupations throughout the Palaeolithic.

The earliest bands of hunters to reach Britain had to contend with extreme climate conditions and there were long episodes when people were completely absent from Britain, during the harshest periods. These human extinctions were then followed by recolonisations. The final extinction of humans came towards the end of the last glaciation and it was only after this that our direct ancestors entered Britain.

The species of humans who have lived in Britain can be described as follows.

Homo antecessor

Evidence for the earliest pre-moderns to reach Europe first came from northern Spain. In 2008, evidence in the form of fragments of a human skull and jaw dating from 1.1–1.2 million years ago, was discovered together with stone tools. That human species has been named *Homo antecessor*, or 'Pioneer Man', a cousin of *Homo erectus*, who evolved into the pre-modern form of *Homo*, which we call *Homo heidelbergensis*.

Homo heidelbergensis

Homo heidelbergensis, or 'Heidelberg Man', evolved in Africa about 600,000 years ago. They subsequently moved out of Africa into Europe, probably alongside the migrations of other mammal species.

A significant development over this timespan was the regular use of fire. The earliest evidence for domestic fire dates to 790,000 years ago in the Jordan Valley. The use of fire was a definitive innovation, which enabled the settlement of new, less optimum landscapes.

By half a million years ago, we can estimate that just a few thousand people dwelled across Europe. Inhabiting mainly river valleys and where animals and plants abounded, they lived in groups of up to probably thirty people. They hunted with long wooden spears and used throwing sticks. *Homo heidelbergensis* was a direct ancestor of Neanderthals.

Homo neanderthalensis

Perhaps the best-known species of pre-modern human is *Homo neanderthalensis*, or 'Neanderthal Man'. Neanderthals became well established in Europe 200,000 years ago. They lived in an often inhospitable dangerous, predator-rich world (outlined in Chapter 4) and brought with them the hunting skills already developed by early humans.

European Neanderthals adapted to a bitterly cold world, where temperatures oscillated dramatically. They were agile, tough and versatile people. Although similar to modern humans in many ways, Neanderthals were a distinct species in their own right. They possessed physical characteristics that enabled them to survive in the colder climate. They were thickset in appearance, with stronger bones, powerful muscles and strong hands and were shorter and stockier than the earlier *Homo heidelbergensis*. Their brain was larger than that of modern humans.

Evidence for Neanderthals in Britain as a whole is still slight and no single bone from one of their skeletons has yet been found anywhere in the country. Evidence is restricted to just a few of their teeth and tools. Even these flint implements are quite scarce. Very few of their occupation sites have been excavated in modern years.

Neanderthals lived alongside modern humans towards the end of their time and there is evidence of interbreeding with modern humans. They finally became extinct about 30,000 years ago.

Homo sapiens

Homo sapiens, or 'modern humans', had evolved in Africa by 200,000 years ago, having diverged as a species from their common ancestors with Neanderthals. Africa's population grew as the colder conditions receded. Initially, small numbers of people began to move beyond that continent.

It is currently thought that there were two significant migrations of modern humans spreading out of Africa. They dispersed over new and often inhospitable terrain. Their descendants moved to the Near East, Eurasia and into Europe. The first movement outwards occurred about 100,000 years ago, while the second push out is dated to about 55,000 years ago.

The Cro-Magnons were the first anatomically modern Europeans. They had fully modern brains and linguistic abilities, coupled with a penchant for innovation.

During the time of modern humans, about 70,000 years ago, we can define a significant development in the human story that we call the Cognitive Revolution. This was a landmark horizon that saw the appearance of the world's first art in the form of ornamental seashells and painting, making use of pigments, such as red ochre.

Homo sapiens spread into Europe about 45,000 years ago, into the heart of the world already occupied by the Neanderthals. The initial settlement of Europe and Eurasia took place when the climate of the north and west of the eastern Mediterranean was briefly warmer.

These modern humans looked at the world in more than practical terms and were able to express themselves in artistic terms, although evidence is now pointing to Neanderthals also having undertaken such activities. Our early ancestors used bone flutes 35,000 years ago, so probably also sang and danced at that time. Before 30,000 years ago, they were creating engravings and paintings on the walls of caves and rock shelters.

Our human story then continues as one of endless ingenuity and adaptability. As people foraged over wide areas, they shared information on food and resources, which would have stimulated the development of more sophisticated communication and fluent speech.

An important innovation of these early people was the apparently simple invention of the eyed needle. This was, in fact, an extremely significant development that allowed them to produce tailored, weather-proof clothing, including fur parkas, long trousers and waterproof boots. They were also good woodworkers. They lived in small hunting bands, often isolated from other communities.

THE FIRST HUMANS IN BRITAIN

Until fairly recent times, it was uncertain just when the first humans found their way to Britain, although it was thought to have been during a warm phase within the Anglian glaciation and probably before about 450,000 years ago. Then, during the early 1980s, a remarkable research project in Sussex revealed one of the world's best-preserved early human sites.

Excavations at Boxgrove produced important evidence for a very early human presence in Britain, in the form of *Homo heidelbergensis*. Work at the site provided a more precise date of between 524,000 and 478,000 years ago. In 1993, the same site produced a single human tibia (shin bone) and two teeth, which remain the earliest human skeletal remains in the whole of north-west Europe. However, as was stated in the introduction to this chapter, discoveries now coming to light along the coast of Norfolk indicate an even earlier date for the arrival of the first humans in Britain, as will be revealed in the next chapter.

Flint Tools

Our evidence for the earliest people in Norfolk comes in the form of their flint tools, which we find in a range of locations, including farmland, gravel quarries and on our beaches. The main tool of the Palaeolithic was the flint handaxe, which was one of humankind's most significant creations and, in a variety of forms, remained in use for about 1 million years. We find these early handaxes in Norfolk in a variety of different shapes and sizes, all of which were carefully crafted to fit comfortably into the hand and had a range of uses.

Despite their name, the main purpose of these axes was not cutting down trees (in fact, there is no evidence for deliberate deforestation or tree removal during the Palaeolithic). These people were hunters, and the axes were for cutting, chopping, skinning and dismembering animal carcasses. When the cutting edges of their tools became blunted through use, they could be resharpened by blows from a hammerstone or piece of antler.

The handaxes were accompanied by other tools, such as scrapers, burins, flakes and points. Other, non-flint, tools were used but they do not survive so well. Bone was employed to make harpoons, multipurpose points and needles. Wooden tools and implements would also have been used.

There are huge differences between the simple handaxes that were made at the start of the Palaeolithic and the more delicately worked flint tools that belong to the end of the Stone Age. The earlier, Upper Palaeolithic way of life had been a very specialised one, essentially geared towards the exploitation of reindeer. Later, modern humans were to develop a more diverse toolkit, employing a range of tools, which reflect adaptations in daily subsistence and the exploitation of new landscapes.

Alone

Initially, our direct ancestors inhabited the same world and interacted alongside the earlier waves of humans who had migrated out of Africa – the Neanderthals, Denisovans and *Homo erectus*. These other hominins died out between 40–30,000 years ago. Until that time, our ancestors had been used to sharing their world with the other species of humans.

Today, we can only imagine what it was like to live alongside such other close relatives, who were similar to us in many ways, but yet different. Would there have been a friendly interaction or hostility? To what extent could they communicate with us? Was there competition for resources between species? Archaeology and science are still searching for the answers to such questions. The scenario conjures up comparisons with the exotic world of J.R.R. Tolkien or even science fiction.

Then, eventually, and for the first time, *Homo sapiens* became the sole surviving member of our genus and alone in the world.

In the next three chapters, we shall follow Norfolk's coastline, initially progressing from the south-east to the north-eastern corner and then westwards, anticlockwise, looking at locations along the Deep History Coast and their significance in relation to the human story, as well as looking at some important historical sites and places that provide more context for the way the coastline has been exploited over time.

First, in the next chapter, we shall look at unique evidence for the presence of the very earliest members of the hominin group who have lived in Norfolk, as we begin our exploration of the coast.

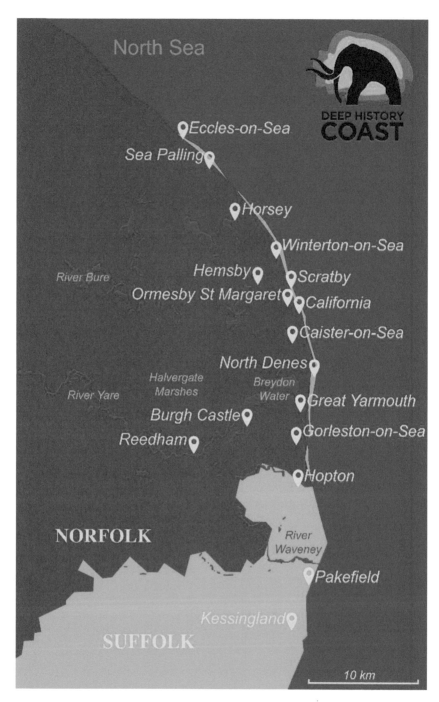

Fig. 15: The coast between Pakefield and Eccles.

6. THE EAST: PAKEFIELD TO WEST RUNTON

THE EASTERN EXTENT OF THE DEEP HISTORY COAST (75KM)

We will begin our exploratory tour of the Deep History Coast in the east of the county, where the coastline is characterised by long and mainly sandy beaches. Much of the east coast is very unstable and susceptible to erosion, especially the stretch to the north of Great Yarmouth, between Hemsby and Trimingham, which has been retreating in some places at the rate of 1.5m per year. Historical records dating from as far back as the seventeenth century tell of significant cliff falls from Happisburgh northwards, which have continuously altered the seaward extent and shape of this coastline.

In the far north-east, the cliffs, which are made from Ice Age Pleistocene sediments, dominate the coastline, starting at Happisburgh, stretching north through Mundesley, then extending west through Cromer, Sheringham and beyond. The geological formation of the Cromer Forest-Bed is also a feature of this stretch and is visible in places. It runs northwards from Covehithe, Suffolk, in the south, and is exposed at Pakefield (also in Suffolk) and West Runton on the north Norfolk coast.

Work now being undertaken off the east coast in relation to the offshore energy industries is providing us with new insights into past, drowned, landscapes situated beyond the shoreline. New wind farms, together with the laying of undersea cables and aggregate extraction, are providing opportunities for the investigation of former land surfaces and the environments inhabited by our distant ancestors. New discoveries are being made, the drowned landscape is being mapped and new sites are being discovered.

That is the setting. In this chapter, we shall explore evidence for the earliest human occupation: the area of true Deep History. We shall see that there is a chronological logic to following the coast from the south-east, northwards and then westwards. This whole stretch of coast is regularly providing fresh evidence for the very earliest prehistoric periods. In this chapter, we shall focus accordingly on the story of the first human presence.

DISCOVERIES ON THE NORTH COAST OF SUFFOLK

Archaeological finds from Norfolk's coast have long pointed to a very early human presence in this part of Britain. For decades, many ancient flint handaxes have been discovered on the coast, from Gorleston and Hopton in the south, northwards to the vicinity of West Runton and beyond in the north, but they have previously lacked good dateable contexts. Although recognised as being Palaeolithic, their precise age has been impossible to determine because of the lack of firm provenances.

However, the suspicion was always that they represented extremely early human activity. Since 2000, further discoveries at secure locations on the coast now confirm that this is, indeed, the case.

The first location to be considered here is, in fact, just beyond Norfolk, in the extreme north-east of Suffolk. A site at Pakefield is integral to the story of the earliest humans; the story that will be continued at the Norfolk sites.

The acidic sandy soils of the Suffolk coast, known as the Sandlings, a landscape of heathland, estuaries, salt marsh and mudflats, lie to the south of the border with Norfolk. At their northern extent, between Kessingland and Pakefield, on the southern edge of Lowestoft, a stretch of cliffs rises above the beach to a height of some 15m. Here, heavy glacial clay deposits

Fig. 16: Pakefield beach, looking south towards the cliffs.

overlie layers of sand, forming cliffs that are ultimately unstable and are now crumbling and revealing important discoveries. Deposits of the Cromer Forest-Bed are being exposed here, beneath Anglian till, where remains of ancient mammals have been found, together with more fragile plant macrofossils and ancient pollen, all of which provide information that allows scientists to reconstruct past environments.

In 2000, an even more remarkable find was made there. A small fragment of flint that had been struck by human hand was discovered in situ within the cliff, inside secure geological deposits. This important observation provided vital proof that humans had been present there much earlier than was previously thought to have been possible, at the time when the Forest-Bed deposits were formed. Other flint tools have subsequently been found nearby and the site and its human presence have now been dated to an amazing 700,000 years ago.

Fig. 17: Pakefield cliffs, showing the Cromer Forest-Bed at the base.

The prehistoric people were at a location adjacent to the estuary of the ancient River Bytham (see Chapter 2). The surrounding landscape at that time embraced areas of grassland, marsh, reeds and alder carr (waterlogged, wooded land). Further afield was deciduous forest. They enjoyed conditions closer to those of the Mediterranean today, with warm summers and mild winters.

At the time of this remarkable discovery, it was evidence for what was then the earliest known human occupation in Britain and also close to the date of the earliest known human presence from the whole of western Europe (which came from Atapuerca in northern Spain). That astonishing situation has since been surpassed by more recent discoveries further north, in coastal Norfolk, which we will encounter later in this chapter.

GREAT YARMOUTH

Progressing along the coast and moving beyond Lowestoft into Norfolk, we first traverse the sandy beaches of Hopton and Gorleston, which are backed by cliffs formed from more glacial sands and gravels. Immediately beyond Gorleston, we reach Great Yarmouth, which is located where Norfolk's Broads meet the sea.

It will be helpful in our exploration of the coastline to look at some sites that do not have a direct association with early prehistory. In fact, we cannot properly undertake a tour of Norfolk's coast without a consideration of some of the towns and villages situated there, in between the major archaeological sites. These places all have historical significance in their own right and cannot be divorced from the broader interpretation of the Deep History Coast.

Great Yarmouth itself has grown up as a long north-to-south, low-lying development, extending for some 4 miles and sandwiched between the River Yare and the North Sea. The town has experienced an unusual history in its relationship with the sea and coast. The land on which it now sits did not exist during the period of Deep History and for much of the prehistoric period the area was under water.

Following the end of the last glaciation, the rivers Yare, Waveney and Bure all drained towards the east, into a large estuary – the area now occupied by Halvergate Marshes. When sea levels rose about 10,000 years ago, during the Mesolithic period, water penetrated further inland. Resulting deposits of clay, sand and silt developed into a sandspit, which formed in the mouth of the estuary. Tidal movements removed this during the Bronze and Iron Ages and there was a vast stretch of open water during the Roman period, which is now referred to as the Great Estuary.

Towards the end of the Roman period and during the Anglo-Saxon era, the sea level fell all around Britain. A sandbank then emerged in the mouth of the Great Estuary, providing new land that was steadily occupied. A settlement grew up there, which eventually became Great Yarmouth.

The first settlement was a seasonal one. Fishermen stayed at the spot as they followed the herring down the east coast of Britain and needed protection from the sea. Their small fishing village, comprising just a collection of huts, grew quickly into a town as the importance of the fishing developed and spread southwards, following the course of the River Yare.

The Domesday Book records Yarmouth in 1086 as a small but vibrant settlement, with a single church and population of about 400. It obtained a charter in 1208 under King John. The town continued to flourish and expand until the middle of the fourteenth century. Its increasing prosperity came from herring fishing and maritime trade.

The instability of the east coast was a constant threat to the prosperity and survival of the town. The coastal sand, which today is one of the town's main attractions, was a threat to the very existence of Yarmouth as a port. By the middle of the fourteenth century, the mouth of the River Yare was becoming unusable, through silting up with sand. Maintaining the town's lifeline to the sea was a struggle that continued over the next 300 years, when seven attempts were made to construct a permanent outlet, each known as a 'haven'.

All of the early attempts to dig a haven silted up after just a few years. It was not until a Dutchman, Joas Johnson, was brought in as engineer on the seventh haven that the problem was eventually solved. The haven that he constructed between 1559 and 1567 remains in use today.

Great Yarmouth developed to become England's eighth most important port and fishing centre, right through until the end of the nineteenth century, during which time the herring fishery continued to grow in importance. The town is currently the second-largest urban centre in Norfolk after Norwich. Its historic prominence in the fishing industry has been extinguished over the years following the Second World War, since when the decline has changed the character of the town. It is now the third-largest holiday resort in the whole country and is the hub for visits to the Broads.

Today, Great Yarmouth is especially important for port-related activities and supporting the offshore oil and gas industries, which are serving to complement the study of the Deep History Coast. Archaeologists now work closely with offshore companies in surveying the seabed for information about the submerged prehistoric landscape. Underwater sites in the vicinity are also being discovered by working with gravel extraction companies. This lost landscape lying beneath the North Sea will be considered further in the next chapter.

NORFOLK'S OFFSHORE WINDFARMS

This stretch of coast is closely associated with the new industry of offshore windfarms, with many already visible off the coastline and others being planned. Norfolk Vanguard was approved in 2020–22 and will be situated 65km out from Bacton. Work on Norfolk Boreas will commence in 2023. The giant Sheringham Shoal farm lies between 17–23km off the north coast, containing eighty-eight wind turbines. Dudgeon sits 32km off Cromer. The Scroby Sands windfarm is situated on the east coast, 3km off Great Yarmouth, where the main operations and maintenance base is located.

THE NORFOLK BROADS

Directly inland from Great Yarmouth, we encounter the flat, watery landscape known as Broadland, which is a prominent feature of east Norfolk where it adjoins the coast. The Broads National Park forms Britain's largest protected area of wetland. It comprises a network of rivers and lakes, covering 303 square km, associated with the natural and navigable rivers Yare, Wensum, Bure, Thurne, Ant, Chet and Waveney.

It is surprising to most visitors to hear that the formation of today's beautiful Broadland landscape was not a natural phenomenon but is essentially the result of early historical industrial activity, in the form of medieval peat workings. Peat was an important source of fuel for the towns of Great Yarmouth and Norwich in early medieval times. The deep deposits in and around the valleys of the rivers draining eastwards into the North Sea were steadily dug out and removed. By the fourteenth century, the peat workings flooded due to sea level changes and the broadland landscape of fen and water, which now characterises east Norfolk, was formed.

Today, this is home to an array of diverse bird, mammal and invertebrate species. In places, it is easy to imagine how the atmospheric Broadland environment echoes the appearance of Norfolk's distant early post-glacial landscape.

BURGH CASTLE AND CAISTER-ON-SEA

As we return to the coast, at this point we come across some more important sites constructed in the early historical period and which are worthy of our attention. We can consider what they are and what their role was in the early exploitation of the coast. These sites of the Roman period, known as forts of the Saxon Shore, still provide an impressive visible legacy for visitors. So, what was the Saxon Shore and what was the function of the sites?

It was during the final century and a half of Roman rule that large walled sites were constructed around Britain's east coast. They have been associated with a defensive system, which has an integral association with Norfolk's coast. This arrangement of forts and signal stations, mainly built during the later third and fourth centuries AD, stretched from Hampshire, eastwards and then northwards to embrace the Norfolk sites of Burgh Castle, Caister-on-Sea and Brancaster, further west.

The fort at Burgh Castle, situated inland from Great Yarmouth, is one of the most spectacular Roman survivals in the east of England. It stands on high ground in a most picturesque setting, some 30m above fenland and the River Yare. Much of the north, east and south walls still stand to a relatively uniform height of approximately 4.6m above the original ground level. The fort has been associated with the name *'Gariannonum'* in the Roman document called the *Notitia Dignitatum*.

The fort stands some distance from the present coastline, although it originally occupied the first landing point on the south side of the Great Estuary. It commanded a safe anchorage and the stretch of water whose outflow to the sea lay through the area now occupied by Great Yarmouth. The walls originally formed a broadly rectangular shape. The long west wall has since fallen away and traces of its surviving masonry have been located in the marshlands below. Externally, the walls are protected by spectacular-looking projecting towers.

The remains of another Saxon Shore fort are located just 7km further north of Great Yarmouth, at Caister-on-Sea. In Roman times, this site lay adjacent to an embayment on the north side of the Great Estuary but is now 1km inland. It appears to have been constructed in the early third century. It was square, with rounded corners and surrounded by two external ditches. The defensive wall originally stood at an impressive 4 or 5m tall, as at Burgh

Fig. 18: Breydon Water at sunset, from the Roman fort at Burgh Castle.

Castle. Much of the site is now obscured by modern housing but the outline of buildings in the vicinity of the south gate have been preserved for visitors to explore.

The Saxon Shore sites would have played a role in safeguarding the vital trade network established on the Great Estuary and other ports along Norfolk's coast. It was at that time that the authority of the Roman Empire was breaking down and external peoples were threatening the stability of Rome's vital trade networks.

It is possible to gain an appreciation of the vastness of the former Great Estuary by visiting the area immediately inland from Great Yarmouth. The expanse of water that is Breydon Water conveys a sense of what the Great Estuary would have looked like. It can best be viewed from Burgh Castle, while its original extent can be gauged from views of the flat grazing marshes visible from the Acle Straight road between the towns of Great Yarmouth and Acle.

CAISTER TO HAPPISBURGH

The stretch of coast to the north of Great Yarmouth is one of beautiful sandy beaches. These are bordered by long stretches of dunes, beginning at North Denes. From here, and extending north beyond Winterton and towards Horsey, is the expanse of slightly higher land that is known as the Isle of Flegg.

Two thousand years ago, Flegg was a distinct island within the northern extent of the Great Estuary. It now lies between the courses of the rivers Bure and Thurne. There has not been a great deal of archaeological investigation on Flegg to date, but we do have evidence for early industry in the form of salt production in the late Iron Age and Roman periods, at Ormesby St Margaret.

On the coastal side of Flegg, the golden-coloured beach is backed by cliffs at California and Scratby. Then, from Flegg's northern extent, the flatlands continue. There are further stretches of dunes through Hemsby, Winterton and Horsey. Heathland has become well established on the landward side here, on the acidic sandy soils.

Fig. 19: The view from the dunes at North Denes, looking north.

Fig. 20: The Winterton-Horsey Dunes, looking south from Horsey.

The dunes between Winterton and Horsey form a natural line of defence against storm and flood waters, although they are noticeably being eroded. They also provide a habitat that encourages a wide range of plants, nesting birds and other animals. In particular, the beach at Horsey is home to a colony of grey seals (*Halichoerus grypus*). The species is essentially an Ice Age remnant. Their pups, not being able to swim immediately, retain a thick white layer of fur that evolved as camouflage during far snowier times. Here, the delicate balance between nature and human interest is apparent, as visitors are drawn to the location to observe the seals, where adults and pups bask on the beach in groups. They can also be observed swimming in numbers just offshore. The seals spend most of their lives at sea, living on a diet of fish and shellfish.

The dunes continue through Horsey, Waxham and Sea Palling to Eccles. Beyond the small village of Waxham and seaward of Sea Palling are human-made defensive reefs, protecting some attractive sandy beaches. Just further north, what was the medieval fishing village of Eccles has become lost to the sea.

Fig. 21   The seal colony at Horsey.

The scouring action of tides occasionally exposes walls, wells and roads of the former settlement. The current village has been protected from further sea incursions by a concrete wall and walkway.

As has been noted above, evidence for prehistoric hunters of the Lower Palaeolithic period, which is the earliest subdivision of the Palaeolithic, before about 300,000 years ago, has been found along this stretch of coast in recent decades. Their flint tools have been discovered at locations including Sea Palling, Eccles, Happisburgh and continuing north to Bacton, Paston, Mundesley, Sidestrand, Overstrand, East and West Runton, Weybourne and Cley-next-the-Sea. Such finds continue to be made.

The handaxe from Eccles beach shown in Figure 2 was discovered in 2004. It was given a probable date of 500,000 years old at that time but could possibly be much older in the light of discoveries that have since been made at nearby Happisburgh, which will be considered in the next section.

Close by, a preserved prehistoric landscape, formed from exposed peats and clays, has been viewed and recorded just off the coast to the north of Waxham. It is unfortunate that, since the construction of offshore rubble reefs intended to protect this fragile coast, these areas are no longer visible. However, earlier aerial photographs revealed a striking landscape with linear features resulting from human occupation, notably in the offshore area between Sea Palling and Eccles. They have been considered to have possible Neolithic and Bronze Age dates.

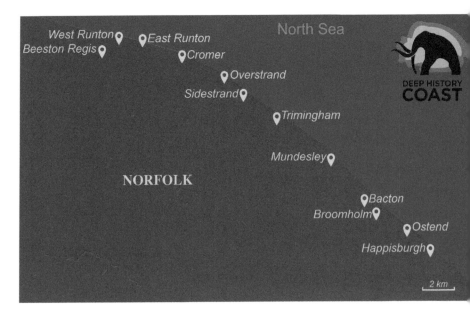

Fig. 22: The coast between Happisburgh and West Runton.

HAPPISBURGH

As we approach the village of Happisburgh, which is readily identifiable from afar by its distinctive red-and-white-banded lighthouse, we observe the coastal topography rising into cliffs. This is unquestionably the most significant location in relation to the importance of the Deep History Coast. The village itself is set back between the higher points of the lighthouse and the church of St Mary. Regular visitors to this location will appreciate the extent to which it is being eroded by the sea and changing dramatically on a steady basis. Of all the stories of Norfolk's coast, it is Happisburgh that has the most to tell. In fact, it could be said that it is here that Britain was born.

The ice sheets of the last glaciation were responsible for shaping this shoreline. Happisburgh is located at the southern end of what are extremely fragile Pleistocene cliffs. Although still reaching some 10m high, they continue to be eaten away by the sea and storms. This is now Europe's fastest-shrinking coast. In just two months in 2003, it was recorded that 13m of coast were lost to the sea.

At the turn of the millennium, discoveries relating to Happisburgh were made that have transformed our knowledge of the very first humans in Europe; illuminating who they were and why they were here. Evidence started to come to light for the presence of very early human activity within the pre-glacial deposits of the Cromer Forest-Bed Formation.

The story began when Simon Parfitt, of the Natural History Museum and University College London, made his discovery during a detailed study of animal bones in their collection, which had been discovered by the Norfolk geologist Alfred Savin (1860–1948). Simon's observation of cut marks on a bison bone betrayed evidence for early human activity in the vicinity of Happisburgh. The delicate human-made scratchings proved that people had been present at that location, where they were cutting up joints of meat to eat, at least half a million years ago.

Shortly after this stunning observation, Mike Chambers made his important discovery of a handaxe at beach level, within a dateable geological deposit, now shown to have been about 500,000 years ago. What is now known as the 'Happisburgh handaxe' is on permanent display in the Natural History Gallery at Norwich Castle Museum and Art Gallery, where visitors can view the object that changed our understanding of the first humans to inhabit Britain.

It is reasoned that the human species responsible for making the Happisburgh handaxe would have been *Homo heidelbergensis*, who had appeared in Africa, Asia and Europe by about 600,000 years ago. *Homo heidelbergensis* had a larger brain than that of the earlier *Homo antecessor*, which may, in turn, have meant a greater intelligence and more developed speech capabilities. The Happisburgh handaxe is a typical *H. heidelbergensis* flint butchery tool dating from about 500,000 years ago and very similar to handaxes found at Boxgrove in Sussex (see Chapter 5).

The discovery of this most important object in situ, together with the cut-marked animal bones, served to stimulate a campaign of further research by the AHOB project team (more recently morphing into the Pathways to Ancient Britain project). Other very early sites nearby have subsequently been discovered and excavated, where more human-struck flints and animal bones were revealed lower down, beneath the current beach level.

The Happisburgh Footprints

In May 2013, severe storms washed away most of the beach sand on the foreshore at Happisburgh, revealing an extensive area of hardened ancient estuary mud from the Cromer Forest-Bed Formation. Members of the Pathways to Ancient Britain team (made up of experts from the British Museum, Natural History Museum, Queen Mary University of London and University of Wales Trinity Saint David) were present in order to try to understand the complex system of estuarine channels there.

Astonishingly, part of the ancient mud surface was seen to be broken by a series of footprints, subsequently dated to at least 850,000 years old. The oldest recorded footprints in Britain had previously been dated to about just 6,600 years old. Following rigorous testing and analysis by the leading UK researchers, it quickly became clear that the Happisburgh footprints were genuinely ancient and therefore not only the oldest human footprints ever recorded in Britain, but the oldest ever recorded outside of Africa.

After being protected by the overlying sediments for almost 1 million years, the Happisburgh footprints were being eroded quickly by the incoming tides. The area was too fragile to excavate successfully and too large to take plaster casts from. It was decided to use multiple digital photographs to create an exact 3D replica model of the footprints. Within two weeks, the original prints had completely eroded away, but the computer modelling revealed forty-nine footprints that had been made by several individuals, varying from 14cm to 27cm in length.

Fig. 23: View of the prehistoric footprint surface at Happisburgh looking north.
(Copyright Simon Parfitt)

Fig. 24: A close-up of one of the prehistoric Happisburgh footprints.

Fig. 25: A reconstruction of the prehistoric site at Happisburgh, 850,000 years ago. (Copyright John Sibbick and AHOB)

We are now almost certain that an adult male who was approximately 1.73m (5ft 9in) tall made the largest footprints, which represent size 9 in today's UK measurements. He was most probably accompanied by an adult female and up to three children. It has been possible to tell that the group were walking in a southerly direction along the estuary, and the children were weaving in, out and around the adults, which is exactly how a family group today might take a walk.

Homo antecessor *in Norfolk*

From the size and age of the prints and the flint tools found nearby, the evidence suggests that the humans who made the Happisburgh footprints were of the species *Homo antecessor*. The age of the site places it close to that of the fossil human material coming from Spain's Gran Dolina, in the Atapuerca complex. It represents some of the earliest evidence for human occupation anywhere in northern Europe.

The stone tools and human footprints from Happisburgh demonstrate that humans first appeared in Britain, on our Deep History Coast, much earlier than had previously been thought possible. Unfortunately, no human bones have yet been found at Happisburgh, although such a discovery remains a very real possibility in the future.

Homo antecessor was a cousin of *Homo erectus*, who had evolved into *Homo heidelbergensis*. *Homo antecessor* would have looked and moved in a very similar way to modern humans. The limited skeletal remains from elsewhere in Europe indicate that males stood approximately 1.72m (5ft 7in) tall and females 1.60m (5ft 3in). Their brain size was about 1,000–1,100cc, while that of modern humans is 1,350cc.

This location about 850,000 years ago was situated adjacent to a slow-flowing river, close to a large estuary. The climate saw temperatures slightly cooler than those of today and closer to those of southern Scandinavia or central Europe. This location was close to a range of different environments including grassland, swamp, reed beds, marshland and freshwater pools. It would have provided people with a diversity of wildlife and natural resources to exploit.

THE COAST FROM HAPPISBURGH TO WEYBOURNE AND THE 'NORFOLK HEIGHTS'

Continuing around the coast from Happisburgh, the land remains higher through the 30km stretch to Weybourne on the north coast, with cliffs still formed from unconsolidated sands and gravels of Pleistocene glacial deposits. Between Mundesley and Trimingham, they reach 50m in height and rise to 70m between Overstrand and Cromer.

Immediately to the north of Happisburgh, a concrete sea wall provides more coastal protection between Ostend and Bacton. Just inland from the seaside village of Walcott and the sandy beach of Bacton stands the historic Bromholm Priory, which was founded in the early twelfth century and later became a destination for pilgrimage of national renown. Today, this part of the coast is known for the Bacton Gas Terminal, located further north at Paston and lying just back from the coast road. This important complex receives gas from fields on the UK continental shelf and a pipeline connects directly to the Netherlands.

Progressing along the coast, 8km from Happisburgh lies Mundesley. The village itself sits on a high point above a beautiful sandy beach, which makes it another popular seaside tourist destination. This was once an important port, although it has always lacked a harbour. Instead, ships and boats have needed to be run ashore onto the beach. Mundesley's cliffs contain Pleistocene sediments of the Cromer Forest-Bed Formation.

Beyond Mundesley, we reach Beacon Hill, where there is a long view towards Overstrand, 4km distant, and across an embayment that contains Trimingham and Sidestrand. Here, we encounter Norfolk's great 'chalk reef' – the Cromer Shoal chalk beds, which emerge from beneath the Crag of the Trimingham cliffs. Among the sands and gravels of the foreshore, the chalk is exposed in a dramatic fashion at low tide, spreading for several hundred metres at beach level. It is interspersed with rows of large black flints in places. The beds are particularly rich in fossils.

Fig. 26: The chalk exposed on the foreshore at Sidestrand.

It is appropriate here to consider this remarkable feature, which is now known to be the longest chalk reef in Britain. Formed over 70 million years ago, it is visible in several places between Trimingham and Cley-next-the-Sea, stretching for some 32km along the north-east coast. At beach level, the chalk beds show as a bright white raft, while further offshore, they contain a range of features, which include tunnels, caves, chalk arches and boulders.

Fig. 27: A band of flint within the chalk on the foreshore at Sidestrand.

This little-known feature provides a unique habitat for biodiversity, providing home to hundreds of species of fish, invertebrates and plant life. It creates a shallow environment, which has become a stable home for animals and plants. These include such strange and wonderful species as the Norfolk purple sponge, the spring squat lobster, the leopard spotted goby fish and beautiful mossy feather weed. It is also responsible for the clean and nutrient-rich waters that produce the flavoursome brown crabs (*Cancer pagurus*) for which Cromer is famous.

The reef's environment is now protected within a Maritime Conservation Zone, which embraces the coastline between Happisburgh and Weybourne. Trawling is prohibited for 3 nautical miles (5.5km) within this zone, out to sea.

Just north of Trimingham, we reach groynes projecting into the sea at Sidestrand, where the adjacent cliffs reach a high point of 60m. Here, spectacular geological processes can be observed in the cliff profile, among the glacial deposits. Chalk rafts containing flints that have been pushed upwards at an angle by the Anglian ice sheet can be seen in the section.

Fig. 28: The cliff at Overstrand, showing chalk rafts pushed upwards by the action of an ice sheet within glacial deposits.

Further north is Overstrand; another village badly affected by coastal erosion and now reinforced by concrete sea defences and a walkway. It is here that the cliffs reach their greatest height, where the Cromer Ridge meets the coast, although they are also eroding at a steady pace. The cliff face is pitted by concave hollows and material comprising glacial sands and clays is regularly deposited on the beach below.

These cliffs contain further spectacular evidence for the power and action of the Anglian ice sheet. Massive chalk rafts are once again clearly visible in the cliff section, where they were forced upwards by the movement of the ice and redeposited. They can be seen positioned beneath Wroxham Crag, Cromer Forest-Bed and Happisburgh till deposits. Close by can be seen the section of a U-shaped channel that cuts into a separate chalk raft and has been filled with sand and flint gravel.

Beyond Overstrand, we follow a sandy beach with patches of stones, especially on the landward side. The wall of cliffs of the Cromer Ridge reach a high point at Lighthouse Hill, from where excellent views of the area can be enjoyed.

CROMER

As we round the north-eastern tip of the county, we approach Cromer, past a row of raised multicoloured beach huts and a view of the town's pier projecting into the sea. The Victorian buildings ahead are dominated by the imposing tower of St Peter and St Paul's Church. Cromer is the largest town in the region. The pier itself was built in 1894 and a prominent lifeboat station was added at its end in 1923. The main town can be reached by steep steps from the beach.

It was during the eighteenth century that Cromer first became a fashionable destination as a bathing resort for visitors. The main period of its development was then in the 1890s. What had been a small fishing village rapidly became one of the most popular

Fig. 29: The view looking east from West to East Runton, with Cromer beyond.

tourist attractions on the east coast. Members of high society were initially drawn to Cromer in search of leisure pursuits and especially its sea bathing. The resort was to become particularly popular among affluent families, who built seaside houses and also large country homes in the vicinity. Today, the town is the main tourist resort on the north Norfolk coast. The beach is a popular destination for families, as well as providing attractive conditions for surfers.

The North Norfolk Visitor Centre at Cromer has recently undergone a refurbishment, with window vinyls proudly stating, 'explorers welcome' and providing information about north Norfolk's section of the Deep History Coast. Cromer Museum sports an informative geology gallery, containing fossil treasures from the Deep History Coast (including parts of the famous West Runton mammoth). Regular Deep History Coast-themed events are run throughout the summer and staff frequently lead groups of school children down to the beach to hunt for fossil sea urchins, belemnites and sponges.

EAST AND WEST RUNTON

As we leave the town, we progress westwards, towards the villages of East and West Runton. On the way, we traverse a slight embayment, where the beach is one of stones and shingle, which can become exhausting to walk across.

Between the villages, the cliffs contain a clear sequence of Pleistocene deposits. Above the beach level, the upper part of the Cromer Forest-Bed Formation is exposed. On top of this are Cromer tills and sands and gravels. It is also possible to see chalk erratics that have been forced upwards by glacial action in the cliff profile.

On reaching West Runton, the cliffs stand at about 10m in height. The higher ground of the Cromer Ridge, inland from West Runton village, is the location of Briton's Lane gravel pit. This provided an important reference site for geologists, revealing a substantial accumulation of sands and gravels, which were deposited at the top of the Cromer Ridge during the Anglian glaciation.

The cliff and beach at West Runton form a location of exceptional interest. The full geological sequence of deposits from successive stages of glacial and interglacial episodes can be viewed in the exposed cliffs.

The top of the chalk is visible once again at low tide at lower beach level. On the foreshore, above the chalk can be found unusual-looking large flints that have distinctive and unusual central voids. These are called paramoudra flints, or 'pot stones', which were formed from the precipitation of silica around a tubular core. Although not fully understood, paramoudra are thought to have developed around a central worm burrow. The worm would have been no thicker than your little finger but, astonishingly, some paramoudra are metres across – formed by a chemical chain reaction that was initiated by the organic matter breaking down within the burrow. The soft bodily remains of this Cretaceous marine worm have never been discovered, but the trace fossil has been given the ichnotaxon name (see glossary on page 164) *Bathicnus paramoudrae*.

Fig. 30: West Runton beach, showing chalk and paramoudra flints on the foreshore.

Fig. 31: The cliff section at West Runton in 2022.

Fig. 32: The Cromer Forest-Bed Formation within the West Runton cliffs. This dark mud and silt layer is often still referred to as the Freshwater Bed in this location.

Above the chalk and paramoudra flints is a thin deposit of the shelly Wroxham Crag, which was formed just before the last ice age. Above the Crag and just above beach level lies a distinctive dark black deposit, which is the upper part of the Cromer Forest-Bed Formation, sometimes known as the Upper Freshwater Bed.

The Freshwater Bed (as referred to in Chapter 3) comprises a 1.5m-thick layer of organic-rich mud and was deposited by a medium-sized, slow-moving river about 600,000–700,000 years ago, immediately before the most extreme cold period of the recent ice age – the Anglian glaciation. It has produced the richest collection of Pleistocene vertebrate faunal remains in the British Isles. The species identified there range from molluscs, beetles, fish, amphibians and reptiles to birds and mammals. It contains thirty-six species of mammal, including shrews, voles, beavers, hyaenas, bears, horses, deer, rhinoceros, mammoths and other elephants. There are also important plant and pollen remains.

Above the Freshwater Bed are sands and silts that span the Cromerian Interglacial period. At the clifftop is the Hanworth till, deposited by the Wolstonian ice sheet (see Chapter 2).

The foreshore from West Runton to adjacent Beeston Regis is distinctive for another feature. Perhaps surprisingly, this represents Norfolk's only true rockpool habitat.

The West Runton Mammoth

A dramatic and truly iconic discovery was made in the cliffs at West Runton in the aftermath of storms that hit the north coast in the winter of 1990. It was through this natural action that the first bones of the West Runton mammoth were exposed. NMS applied for funding to excavate what was obviously a very important find and to recover as much of the skeleton as had survived in the Cromer Forest-Bed Formation. Excavation took place in 1995 and the surviving skeleton, recovered by the excavation, was found to be approximately 85 per cent complete.

Fig. 33: Excavation of the West Runton mammoth in 1995, showing a tusk *in situ*.

The huge animal belonged to the species *Mammuthus tro-gontherii*, which is also known as the steppe mammoth (see Chapter 4). It is perhaps more accurately described as a 'giant forest mammoth'. It stood at least 4m at the shoulder and would have weighed about 10 tonnes – twice the weight of today's African elephant. This is the largest elephant skeleton ever found in Britain and was probably one of the biggest animals ever to have lived on land, except for the very largest dinosaurs.

It is also the oldest elephant skeleton to have been found in the UK, although some older individual teeth and bones do exist. Only a few other skeletons of this species are known, coming from Germany, Serbia and Russia.

Elephant or Mammoth?
Initially, people referred to West Runton's mammoth as the 'West Runton elephant'. More recently, it has been called the 'West Runton mammoth' – so which is correct? The answer is that they are technically both right, as a mammoth is just a type of elephant.

When the fossilised remains were first found, it was briefly thought that they might belong to another extinct species called a straight-tusked elephant (*Palaeoloxodon antiquus*). Then, when it was discovered that it was a steppe mammoth, some people still called it an elephant, in order not to confuse it with the smaller, hairier woolly mammoth. These days, we all tend to call it the West Runton mammoth, which is a much more specific and accurate term.

At West Runton, ancient water beetles recovered during the excavation (see Chapter 4), tell us that about 700,000 years ago, slow-moving water meandered through the area. The beetles would have fed on decomposing vegetation such as duckweed and water lilies. A little further away, there were beetles that favour trees such as oak, elm, hazel, spruce and pine. Others thrived in dry-ground vegetation, such as heather and grassy glades, all revealing the range of habitats in the vicinity at that period of Deep History.

Fig. 34: A Norfolk landscape during the Cromerian Interglacial, between 900,000 and 500,000 years ago by Nick Arber. (Copyright Norfolk Museums Service).

THE RECOLONISATION OF BRITAIN: NEANDERTHALS IN NORFOLK

As has been explained in Chapter 5, the human occupation of Britain has not been a continuous one. At times, during the Ice Age, this country has been too cold to sustain human life. There were long periods when humans were not present. Once again, evidence from Norfolk has played an important role in understanding the national story.

Britain was completely deserted for a huge expanse of time between 180,000 and approaching 65,000 years ago. At the end of that period, humans in the form of Neanderthals finally returned to Britain.

In order to complete this story, we must make a short detour inland to a site at Lynford, in the Breckland, which has provided evidence for the earliest human presence in the country, after an absence of 115,000 years.

Lynford is located in Thetford Forest, where a group of gravel pits sit within a flood plain terrace on the south bank of the River Wissey. These gravels were deposited during the Ice Age. It was during gravel extraction in 2002 that a number of woolly mammoth teeth were discovered in association with a beautiful black flint handaxe, in perfect condition, within the same layer of sediment, having lain undisturbed for tens of thousands of years. Significantly, the handaxe was of the bout-coupé form – a distinctive tool used only by Neanderthals. This Neanderthal presence was later dated to between 64,000 and 67,000 years ago; approximately 30,000 years before the first modern humans arrived in the British Isles.

The site at Lynford had been located beside a river, where both large mammals and predators had come to drink. The Lynford Neanderthals lived in temporary shelters to protect them within what was then a hostile, cold and open landscape. We can see how they used their flint tools to cut meat from the huge carcasses, at what is a very rare example of a mammoth butchery site in the British Isles. Altogether, the remains of at least nine woolly mammoths (*Mammuthus primigenius*) were found, including one juvenile animal. The Neanderthals probably used their handaxes to cut away the large meat-bearing bones, which were then taken to a safe distance to eat, away from other predators that were visiting the site to drink.

Four Species of Humans

Norfolk now has evidence for the presence of more species of humans than any other part of Britain. *Homo antecessor* and *Homo heidelbergensis* have been evidenced on the Deep History Coast and *Homo neanderthalensis* inland at Lynford. All of them made stone tools, mostly from flint. They each had their own particular manufacturing styles and 'toolkits', so we can often tell by the shape of the tools to which species they belonged. Together with modern humans, *Homo sapiens*, Norfolk has evidence for four species of humans having lived within its borders.

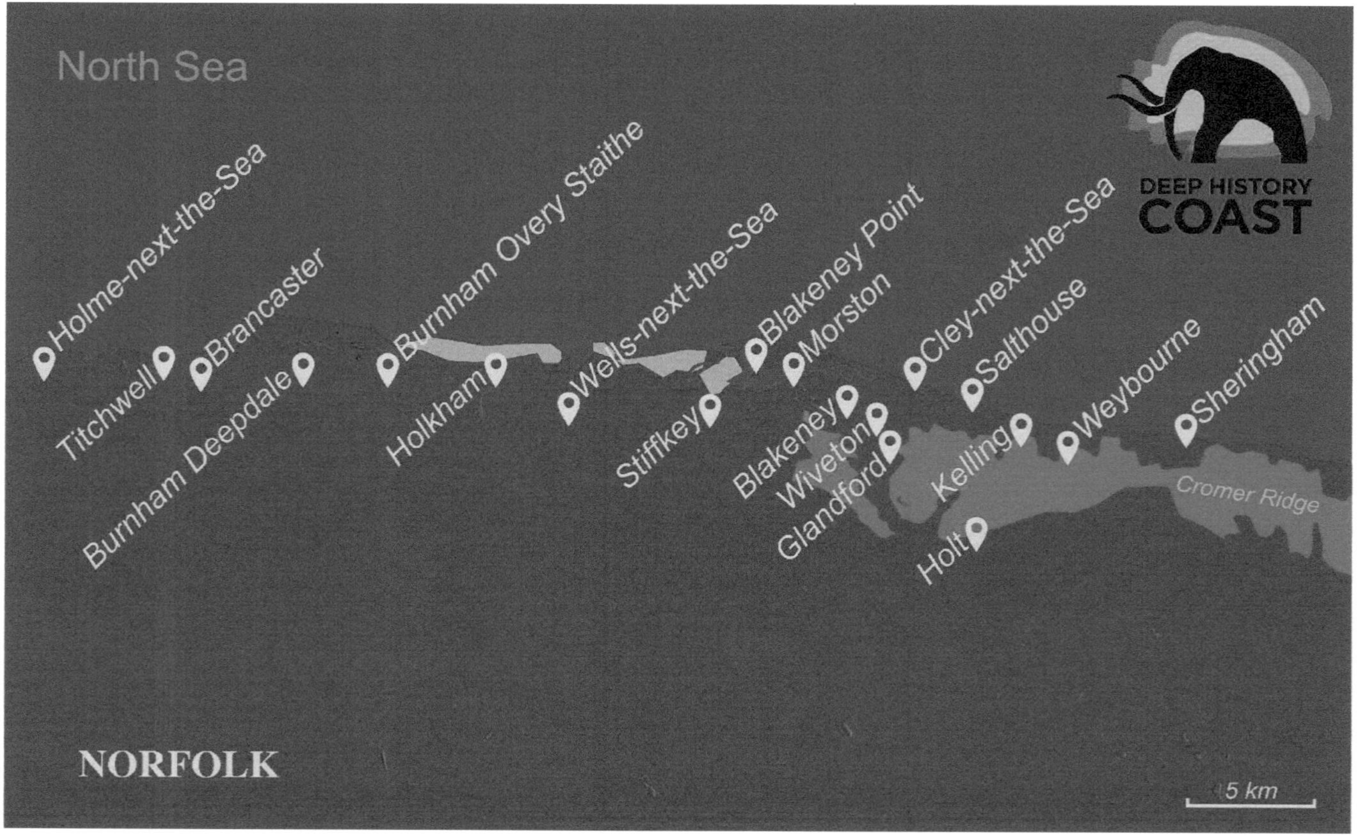

Fig. 35. The coast between Sheringham and Holme

7. THE CENTRAL NORTH COAST: SHERINGHAM TO HOLME

THE CENTRAL PART OF THE DEEP HISTORY COAST (45KM)

As we reach the north Norfolk coast, we enter a dynamic landscape of changing coastal formations. The longshore wave direction here is westwards and is responsible for dune erosion and recession in some places, which is coupled with coastal deposition in others. These processes contrast with that of the cliff erosion previously encountered on the east and north-east coast.

In this stretch, the cliffs of the 'Norfolk Heights' give way to low-lying beaches and marshes. Long shingle spits and stretches of dunes are backed by salt marsh and mudflats inland, all of which are continually being shaped and reshaped by the sea. This part of the coast is characterised by what are termed 'barrier' beaches, which form a gentle offshore slope, beneath shallow waters, together resulting in a relatively lower wave energy.

During the summer months, the north coast is susceptible to a chilly mist that rolls in from the North Sea. Known as a sea fret, this cold fog is caused by warm air, normally between the months of April and September, passing over the cold sea. The frets are restricted to the coastal strip and can continue while, nearby, conditions inland are warm and sunny. Norfolk's sea frets are responsible for favourable growing conditions for cereal production across the area.

Following this stretch of coast will enable us to look at the later episodes of prehistory, relating to the post-glacial period. In this chapter, we shall be introduced to the settlement of Norfolk during the Mesolithic, Neolithic and Bronze Age. There is a great deal of current research into these periods, notably through offshore archaeology in relation to the mapping of the North Sea bed, across the expanse we now refer to as Doggerland.

DOGGERLAND

For most of its prehistory, our country has not been an island. Britain was joined to the continent of Europe and the sea lay far to the north of its current position. The coast was far away, forming a line running from the current Yorkshire coast to the northern tip of Denmark. Britain was effectively a peninsula of Europe.

During the period of the last Cold Stage of the Devensian glaciation, a large part of Britain, together with much of what is now the North Sea, was covered in ice. The sea level was about 120m lower. Other parts of Britain and the North Sea were covered with tundra.

The northern coastline was backed by a landscape of lagoons, salt marsh, rivers and lakes. This environment provided the inhabitants with a bounty of resources for fishing, eating shellfish and hunting wildfowl.

Behind the coast was a large fertile plain, which was populated by vast herds of animals on a scale that is seen on Africa's Serengeti plain in modern times and providing rich hunting grounds. It was named 'Doggerland' by Professor Bryony Coles in the 1990s, during her pioneering study of this landscape.

At the end of the Devensian cold period, the huge glaciers melted and the sea level rose. Then, as the weight of the ice lessened, the land started to tilt and dry land became submerged under the North Sea. What had previously been a peninsula of Europe was cut off and Britain became an island just 8,500 years ago. The enormous landscape of Doggerland was drowned.

Today, as fishing boats cast their nets, alongside the catches of cod, sole and turbot, they regularly turn up bones and teeth of creatures that once roamed this great plain. Fishermen have dredged up many tonnes of bones of giant extinct animals from the seabed. Remains of woolly mammoth, woolly rhinoceros, wild horse and bison have been recovered in very large quantities from depths in excess of 20m, reflecting the sheer numbers of creatures that once roamed this expanse. This was once a very rich terrestrial environment. In the wake of the herds, we also have evidence of predators, which included lions and hyaenas.

Doggerland is now the focus of intense archaeological interest and investigation. However, the study of this submerged landscape presents a unique set of difficulties and new archaeo-geophysical techniques are being developed, alongside the application of computer modelling and molecular biology. These investigations look at the nature of past environments, ecological change and the nature of early human communities. The new information is being used to identify where people were and where archaeology might survive within this massive landscape.

Doggerland is providing us with one of the most exciting archaeological landscapes for study anywhere in Europe. Unfortunately, it is difficult for non-specialists to engage with the kind of work being undertaken from ships and by divers, both in the deep sea and in the closer intertidal zone. Over the coming years, it will be possible to produce models of the original landscape and to explore the lost terrain through computer graphics that more of us can better understand and share.

In the meantime, we can view some surviving remains of Doggerland's forests at intervals along the Deep History Coast. There are a number of locations where stumps of ancient trees can be seen at low tide. These include sites at Titchwell, Gore Point and Holme-next-the-Sea in the north and Sea Palling in the east. Researchers have also identified a number of very fragile archaeological sites that still survive within the intertidal zone and are exposed at low tide, together with others located further beyond the current coastline.

SHERINGHAM

Continuing our exploration along the coast from West Runton, the high ground at Beeston Hill slopes down towards a harbour and seafront at Sheringham. The town originally grew in importance through its role in coastal fishing. Much of its development belonged to the years from the 1890s to the early twentieth century. It is now a popular seaside resort, in tandem with nearby Cromer. The adjacent Sheringham Park, further inland, is another popular draw for locals and tourists from afar.

The 1,000 acres of Sheringham Park are in the care of the National Trust. The park was originally designed by the famous landscape architect Humphrey Repton (1752–1818). Famous today for its displays of azaleas and other rhododendrons, it combines woodland walks and unequalled panoramic views of the coast, especially from its treetop viewing platform. It also contains the grand Sheringham Hall, again the work of Repton and constructed between 1812 and 1817, which is not open to the public.

Fig. 36: The view towards Sheringham from Kelling Heath.

Sheringham Museum at the Mo, situated on the seafront, contains an eclectic mix of local lifeboats and fishing boats, photographs and glass negatives, boatbuilding tools, paintings and drawings. It also houses a collection of fisherman's woollen sweaters, called ganseys, and there is a display of local fossils from along the Deep History Coast.

THE CROMER RIDGE

A sense of the scale of what was once Doggerland can be experienced by looking out to sea from high points just inland, including those inside Sheringham Park and the adjacent Kelling Heath. In fact, the best raised locations belong to the geological feature known as the Cromer Ridge, which dominates the landscape along this part of the coast. The ridge stretches inland from the area between Mundesley and Cromer, rising to over 100m south of Sheringham. It forms one of the highest locations across the whole of East Anglia. The ridge then continues inland, to the south of Holt, extending for 14km in length, almost through to Thursford.

The Cromer Ridge is a glacial feature, created during the Anglian Cold Stage, 470,000–400,000 years ago. It was formed from glacial moraines, scoured from the bed of the North Sea and deposited along the edge of a great ice sheet at this point. The ridge therefore serves to indicate the extent of the ice at a point in time and represents a pause in the flow of the sheet, depositing hundreds of thousands of tonnes of material along the way.

Several other associated features resulting from glacial action can also be seen here. These include a formation known as an esker, located on the Wiveton Downs, which is a long sand and gravel ridge running for 3.5km between Blakeney and Glandford. What is known as the Blakeney Esker was originally formed within a channel cut into the base of the ice. This is perhaps the finest example of such a glacial feature in England.

Fig. 37: The Blakeney Esker glacial outwash feature at Glandford, situated to the south of Blakeney and Cley.

Just to the east, at Kelling Heath and Salthouse Heath can be found associated glacial outwash plains. Formed from sand and gravel sediments, these landscapes indicate the position of the front of the ice sheet, having been formed from deposits carried by meltwater streams at the front of the glacier, which also contained the Blakeney Esker. Further erosional remnants of the glacial outwash plain can be seen as raised mounds along the coast near Salthouse, at Great Hulver Hill and Scrib Hill.

As we progress further west, we encounter some more recent prehistoric sites, which lead us into the post-glacial Holocene epoch. Our starting point will be those of the Mesolithic period.

The Mesolithic in Norfolk

This part of the coastline enables us to consider later prehistoric periods, through sites of interest in the area. We shall begin in the vicinity of Sheringham and then move further along the north coast, with an initial explanation of these periods.

The period following the Palaeolithic, from about 10,000 BC, is known as the Mesolithic. At that time, the last northern ice sheets were melting and sea levels were rising. The relatively large human population that had been drawn to the Doggerland plain by its abundant wildlife and natural resources needed to move inland, in both directions, as Britain became cut off.

An increase in air temperature meant areas that had previously been tundra could now be colonised by more plants. Forest spread right across the Norfolk landscape. The open steppe-tundra of the Ice Age gave way to a woodland of birch, then pine and finally broadleaf forest. The predominant trees were oak, elm, hazel, lime, ash and maple. There was also hornbeam, yew and pine. Animal species were also changing with the developing climatic conditions.

People and animals steadily returned to the area from further south as conditions became warmer. Norfolk became occupied by small groups of mobile hunters and gatherers, who exploited the abundant wildlife that was all around them in the woodlands, marshes, sea and rivers. The homes of these people were temporary structures constructed from trees, branches and wooden stakes. People also made good use of organic material resources such as wood and reeds to make tools and utensils for everyday use. They were a society of skilled people, who worked wood and flint to a very high standard. They constructed log boats, which were paddled along Norfolk's rivers and streams. They made bows, spears and harpoons for hunting. Fishing was assisted by the use of nets and fish traps.

There is little surviving evidence for Mesolithic settlements. Most of what we have is in the form of their flint tools, which are most often found on sandy soils next to rivers. One of the richest deposits comes from Kelling Heath, which will be described below.

The Transition to the Neolithic

The Mesolithic was succeeded by the period known as the Neolithic. The most significant change was the transition from the hunter-gatherer lifestyle to one that was based on farming.

Neolithic settlements are generally found in East Anglia from about 4300 BC.

It is from this time that we find more visible remains of a human presence in the landscape. Occupation sites and monuments are found right along the coast. Some constructions remain, in the form of earthworks, while cropmarks reveal the existence of extensive prehistoric landscapes where people lived.

The people living on the east coast of Britain continued to have cultural ties and contact with the population of the near continent, based on relationships stretching back to before the flooding of Doggerland. As new ideas reached those parts of northern Europe there was little delay in their reaching eastern Britain. In this way, communities living in the area of Norfolk were some of the first people in Britain to adopt the new farming lifestyle that spread across Europe (see Chapter 4).

SHERINGHAM TO SALTHOUSE

Continuing our coastal exploration and leaving Sheringham, we approach Weybourne. The Weybourne cliffs exhibit a clear sequence of Anglian glacial deposits, which lay above gravelly Wroxham Crag and, in turn, overlie chalk bedrock.

At Weybourne, the topography dramatically changes character. The higher ground suddenly falls away and the beach becomes pebbly. Here, at the location called Weybourne Hope, is the start of the shingle spit leading west to its eventual terminal at Blakeney Point. It is also from here that the beach gives way to a shoreline of salt marsh behind shingle ridges and offshore sand and shingle bars, which then stretch all the way to Holme in the far north-west.

Fig. 38: The cliffs at Weybourne, looking south from Weybourne Hope.

Fig. 39: The beach, looking north from Weybourne Hope.

Just inland from here is the village of Kelling, which is backed by the higher Kelling Heath, extending over some 10km and made from glacial sands and gravels that are integral to the story of the Deep History Coast. The surrounding area can best be viewed from Telegraph Hill, from where the heath shelves steeply to the north and west, with a lesser incline to the south.

The surrounding landscape contains many remnants of its glacial past, which have been described above. There are also magnificent views, both inland and outwards to the coast and sea. This is a significant location in relation to the Mesolithic and Neolithic periods.

The important Early Mesolithic site on Kelling Heath is one of the richest deposits known from that period in Norfolk. Prolific scatters of flint artefacts are spread over a large area. The prime location is just 2km inland from the north coast. Its naturally high position on the top of the Cromer Ridge would have provided hunters with a magnificent view for miles across the great Doggerland plain. From here, they could view migrating herds of deer and other animals, as well as passing groups of people.

Unfortunately, the acidic soil conditions at Kelling have not preserved anything other than flints, which have survived in large numbers. The hundreds of tiny flint microlith points would possibly have been used to repair hunting tools such as spears and arrows.

Looking back towards the coast from here, the imposing landmark of Muckleburgh Hill stands out prominently on the beachline. This is another distinctive glacial formation; a mound, formed from sands and gravels, which was originally deposited within a retreating glacier. This kind of formation is known as a kame.

As we continue our journey west, we pass the Muckleburgh Collection, which is one of the largest privately owned military museums in the country. Here, we might encounter historic military vehicles giving rides or displays to visitors, within sight of the beach.

Introducing the Later Neolithic and Bronze Age

Sea levels remained high through the Neolithic period before eventually falling in the Bronze Age. This was a period of favourable climate, with conditions that were warmer and drier than those of today. The farming communities steadily spread their new way of life across the Norfolk landscape.

The period of the Later Neolithic, which can be dated from about 3200 BC, saw more significant developments in society. The people left evidence of their presence in the form of large visible monuments in the landscape, many of which either still survive or can be traced through archaeology. These monuments required the cooperation of large numbers for their construction. The evidence for social cooperation on such a scale only occurred following the stability provided by the Agricultural Revolution of the Neolithic.

Monuments known as causewayed enclosures take their name from the interrupted ditch circuits that surround them. Two of these rare sites have been identified close to the north Norfolk coast. One has been located by aerial photography at Salthouse, next to Kelling, and another a little further inland at Roughton, to the south of Cromer. These are both small examples in national terms, surrounded by single ditches. The latter is set within a whole landscape of Neolithic and Bronze Age monuments, with long and oval barrows and mortuary enclosures close by. The monuments would have been used as meeting places for their surrounding communities. It has also been proposed that they may have been located at the centre of territories of early farming groups.

It was from about 2500 BC that bronze was first used across Britain and we enter the age of metals. The introduction of metalworking was a considerable improvement on flint-working technology. Objects of early Bronze Age date are well represented in Norfolk. Their findspots confirm that the eastern edge of the fens, in the south-west of our Deep History Coast, was a major regional concentration of bronze-working and settlement.

Large numbers of Bronze Age round barrows have been recorded on or near to Norfolk's coastline. They are best seen through aerial photography and not all survive above ground level. Most have been levelled and survive only as ring ditches. Round barrows are most numerous in the central and north-eastern parts of the north Norfolk coast, especially on the heaths, including those at Kelling, Roughton and Salthouse.

Burial mounds such as these frequently occur in cemetery groups. There are at least nine barrows on Kelling Heath, which are arranged in two parallel lines and are bisected by a trackway. The largest barrow group known in Norfolk is at nearby Salthouse Heath, which is thought to have been used for a lengthy period of 2,000 years, spanning the Late Neolithic and Bronze Age.

Fig. 40: Looking across Norfolk's largest group of prehistoric barrows, situated on Salthouse Heath, which were in use for over 2,000 years, between the Late Neolithic and Bronze Age. These burial mounds are now well hidden by trees.

SALTHOUSE WESTWARDS

Continuing along the coast from Weybourne, we have noted that the topography subsides into a lower stretch of marshland. We reach the village of Salthouse, which was once a port but is now set back behind marshes, which are, in turn, land-locked by the coastal shingle bank. Flints of both the Palaeolithic and Mesolithic periods have been found here.

From Salthouse to Holme-next-the-Sea, in the far north-west, salt marshes skirt much of the coastline. Whereas the story of much of Norfolk's coast has been one of erosion, the salt marshes represent the opposing phenomenon of deposition. The erosion seen on other stretches results in the transport and deposition of sediment to these parts. The marshes and shingle bars from Scolt Head to Thornham are just such an area of coastal deposition.

There are two more coastal sites between Wells and Cromer that may be associated with the Roman Saxon Shore system, which was described in the previous chapter. This time, they are not forts, like those at Burgh Castle and Caister-on-Sea. They are platforms located in raised positions that provided clear views of the surrounding land and sea and appear to have served as signal stations, established between the forts. They would have originally had structures on top and probably supported beacons or semaphore stations.

The first of these is at Warborough Hill, Stiffkey, where a mound forms an artificial platform, capped by layers of mortared flint, although much of the original surface has been robbed away. At Gramborough Hill, Salthouse, is another isolated mound, located on the beach between Salthouse and Weybourne. Its construction bears similarity to the Stiffkey site. It is square in plan with a flat top. A ditch was originally recorded on the seaward side, which has since been removed by sea action. The pronounced glacial feature of Muckleburgh Hill at Kelling is much higher. A Roman site has been identified on its top and it has been speculated that this too might have been used as a signal station.

Fig. 41: The Roman platform at Gramborough Hill, Salthouse.

THE GLAVEN PORTS WESTWARDS

To the west of Salthouse and inland from a stretch called the Fresh Marshes lie villages that are collectively known as the Glaven Ports. In historical times, Cley, Wiveton and Blakeney together provided safe anchorage on the exposed north coast. Trade and commerce thrived there from the thirteenth century and they remained important through the medieval period, primarily as fishing ports and secure bases for longshore fishermen. The catches grew in size and fish were salted and exported from here. Although principally engaged with fishing, other important regional products also passed through the ports including salt, wool and local agricultural produce.

A combination of silting rivers and enclosed marshes caused the eventual decline of the Glaven Ports, which are now separated from the sea by the marshes. Their decline saw the rise of ports further west, at Wells-next-the-Sea and King's Lynn. However, parts of the Glaven Valley remained tidal until the early nineteenth century.

Today, the village of Cley-next-the-Sea is readily identified by its distinctive windmill and winding streets. It is now a renowned focus for bird watching and, in turn, is the main place where birders choose to congregate. Blakeney is another beautiful village, where small boats can still access its picturesque quayside from the sea, via Blakeney Point.

On the seaward side of Cley and Blakeney and beyond the Fresh Marshes is the shingle and sand spit of Blakeney Point. This has been formed by the process of littoral drift (see glossary, page 164). The eastern end starts at the termination of the higher coast at Weybourne and extends for 15.5km to its far western end, just seaward of Morston and Stiffkey. The spit is formed from a shingle bank with dunes at the headland. This was Britain's first coastal nature reserve, established in 1912. It is now home to the country's biggest permanent colony of common (*Phoca vitulina*) and grey (*Halichoerus grypus*) seals.

Fig. 42: Looking towards the coastal village of Blakeney across the salt marshes.

Fig. 43: The view north towards Blakeney Channel from the village.

Just a mile further west is the small fishing village of Morston, lying inland from a landscape of mature salt marshes to the south of Blakeney Point. This was another major port during the medieval period, remaining important until just 400 years ago. Today, it provides a base for tourists looking to embark on seal-watching trips. An example of a raised beach can be found here, in which sediments deposited about 185,000 years ago have been lifted and exposed.

Next to Morston is the village of Stiffkey, which is famous for its seafood and, in particular, its cockles, which are known as 'Stewkey Blues'. A 3km stretch of the coastline embracing Stiffkey Marsh and Warham Marsh are in the care of the National Trust and provide an important winter breeding ground for birds.

Fig. 44: Warham salt marshes, to the north of Wells.

The small town of Wells-next-the-Sea is situated 10km west of Stiffkey, again separated from the sea by salt marsh, but it retains its access to the sea and its role as a port. Wells was another medieval sea port and remained important until the sixteenth century, with corn as its main export. It was later famous for malting in the nineteenth and early twentieth centuries.

To the north and east of the harbour, a sea wall was built to protect agricultural land to the west from the sea in the mid-nineteenth century. The still-busy harbour is connected to the sea by a channel called the Run. The adjacent sandy beach is now one of the major tourist focuses of the north Norfolk coast.

Fig. 45: The entrance to Wells Harbour.

Immediately to the west of Wells lie some of the most magnificent and extensive beaches of the whole coast, which stretch to Holkham and then through to the Burnhams. The gently shelved beach at Holkham Bay is backed by dunes that reach approximately 15m in height. Behind the dunes is a distinctive strip of Scots pines, established to provide protection on the landward side from prevailing winds.

Situated just inland from here is the Holkham Estate. Holkham Hall is one of finest examples of the Palladian style in the whole of the country and its design shows the strong influences from classical Roman architecture. The house was built for Thomas Coke, 1st Earl of Leicester (1697–1759), by the architect William Kent (1685–1748), who is recognised as having introduced the Palladian style into England.

Fig. 46: The extensive open beach at Holkham beneath a wintry sky.

The name of the later Thomas Coke, 1st Earl of Leicester (1754–1842), is associated with advances in British agriculture. Coke took a major interest in his park and gardens, planting extensive areas of woodland. He also employed Humphrey Repton, designer of Sheringham Park, to modify the design of the grounds and gardens, which are another popular tourist destination today.

Some 4km further west from Holkham Hall is Burnham Overy Staithe. Here, the village provides access to Scolt Head, a sand and shingle island stretching for over 5km, covered by sand dunes and backed by salt marsh and a network of creeks. This formation developed over 10,000 years ago as glacial outwash. It is now a National Trust and Norfolk Wildlife Trust nature reserve, providing a haven for birds, insects, land and marine mammals and an environment for rare flora.

BRANCASTER TO HOLME-NEXT-THE-SEA

Travelling 4km west from Burnham Overy Staithe is Brancaster Staithe, which retains a harbour and outlet to Brancaster Bay. Just inland lies Burnham Thorpe, the birthplace of Admiral Lord Nelson (1758–1805). Then, 6km west of Burnham Overy Staithe lies Brancaster village, which is separated from the sea by Mow Creek and an area of salt marsh.

Today, the site of a former Roman presence at Brancaster, another of the Saxon Shore forts introduced in Chapter 6, lies on a slight elevation above salt marshes, where there has been much silting since the medieval period. A combination of salt marshes, creeks and dunes have formed between the site and Brancaster Bay.

In the Roman period, a fort here would have stood beside a navigable inlet with a sheltered anchorage, protected from the North Sea by a spit of land. Nothing of the fort remains above ground level today, although historical records state that the walls were standing to a height of 12ft as recently as 1600. The site has been revealed to us today through a combination of aerial photography, ground survey and partial excavation.

The fort was almost square, with rounded corners, enclosing 2.6 hectares. Unlike Burgh Castle, there is no evidence for external bastions. The walls were built of sandstone, with a flint, ironstone and chalk-rubble core. The building materials came mainly from local sources. Chalk came from quarries in the west, near the shores of the Wash, while flint came from coastal parts of north Norfolk.

Although nothing remains above ground today, grey stone blocks from the fort can be seen built into the chancel of the nearby church of St Mary the Virgin at Brancaster and in other local churches, including St Mary's at Burnham Deepdale and St Mary the Virgin at Titchwell. They are also found in houses, farm buildings and walls in the villages of Brancaster and Brancaster Staithe.

To the west of Brancaster and 9km north-east of Hunstanton is the village of Titchwell. On the seaward side is a prominent RSPB nature reserve, covering 170 hectares, where species including the bittern (*Botaurus stellaris*) can be heard – and sometimes even observed! Another rich site of Mesolithic date has been discovered here, at its intertidal extent. The reserve is visited by many thousands of birders every year, most of whom are totally unaware that this beautiful natural landscape was a focus of human and not just avian activity some 9,000 years ago.

The early settlement at Titchwell spanned the Late Glacial and Early Mesolithic periods, following the recession of the last ice sheet from this area. At that time, this was another open, inland site, possibly situated close to a river, which could have attracted people to this specific location. They may also have been attracted by the availability of good-quality flint, which was exposed in the till. This is also perhaps the best location for seeing fragments of Doggerland's ancient forests on the beaches.

Archaeological fieldwork at Titchwell revealed a flint industry based on blade production, which is a very distinctive form of Mesolithic industry. Similar flint tool types have been found along the nearby beach, between Thornham and Brancaster, but in smaller numbers. It is possible that they are indicators of other similar sites of the same period that also lie within intertidal deposits.

The marshes of Titchwell extend westwards to Thornham. The coastline remains low at this point, becoming dunes through to Holme-next-the-Sea. Thornham was another medieval port that is now cut off from the sea by salt marsh and sandy beach.

In the far west, situated 5km north of Hunstanton, is the small village of Holme-next-the-Sea. Here, a shingle and sand ridge and dunes have formed to the north of the village and continue round to Hunstanton. Holme Marshes have developed landwards, behind the ridge and in its shelter. This is another important location for migratory birds. Holme is home to two nature reserves, which are owned by the Norfolk Wildlife Trust and the Norfolk Ornithological Association. It is here that the ancient road called the Peddars Way meets the Norfolk Coast Path, which together form a national trail for walkers. Holme is now more famous for another archaeological site that also dates from that period.

Fig. 47: The shingle and sand ridge and dunes backing the beach to the north of Holme village, just south of Gore Point.

The Peddars Way

The Peddars Way was an ancient road through central-west Norfolk. It runs northwards from Bildeston in Suffolk, cutting through Norfolk's Breckland and passing through Threxton, reaching the coast at Holme-next-the-Sea in the extreme north-west. It has been suggested that this terminal point might have been a ferry location for vessels in the Roman period, perhaps of military origin, to cross the Wash into Lincolnshire. The Peddars Way might have been constructed by the Romans, possibly in the aftermath of the Boudican rebellion, after AD 61, although it may have had even earlier origins, possibly as far back as the Bronze Age.

Seahenge

A form of wooden monument, as yet unique to Norfolk, was identified at Holme-next-the-Sea in 1998 (see Figure 6). It had been exposed due to erosion of the sand dunes. Although the location of this mysterious timber structure is on the coast, at the time of its construction it was further inland, within an area of salt marsh. Its purpose remains uncertain and has become a focus of continuing fascination.

Despite its popular name, it was not a henge monument. A true henge can be defined as a form of round enclosure consisting of a bank that lay beyond an internal ditch. Instead, this Norfolk structure comprised an oval arrangement of oak posts surrounded by an upside-down central oak stump. There were fifty-six posts, which had each been split in half, with their flat surfaces facing inwards, creating a flat inner wall. It had a single entrance, which faced south-west, aligned towards the midwinter sunset. It has been calculated that 200 people may have been involved in its construction. Modern scientific techniques have dated the timbers very precisely to 2049 BC.

Fig. 48: Holme dunes and beach, close to the location where Seahenge was discovered.

So, what could the purpose of Seahenge have been? One possibility is a form of mortuary structure, inside which a dead body would have been exposed. Alternatively, it could have served as a shrine.

Seahenge is a unique form of monument in national terms and may represent a regional form of Bronze Age structure. It is difficult to interpret this construction in isolation and it may have originally been strategically situated within a wider ritual landscape. In fact, a second similar timber circle was identified just 100m to the east, although this was never excavated and has since been lost to the elements. Future discoveries in the area and a fuller appreciation of the local prehistoric landscape may provide more clues towards their original function in the future.

The oak posts and central stump of Seahenge have been preserved and can be viewed at the Lynn Museum, King's Lynn. Here, they have been arranged in a partial reconstruction of the monument, together with more information about the Bronze Age period and the prehistoric landscape.

8. THE WEST: HUNSTANTON TO THE WASH

THE WESTERN PART OF THE DEEP HISTORY COAST (25KM)

Leaving Holme-next-the-Sea, we pass Gore Point and turn south, where the western extremity of the Deep History Coast follows a transition from sand dunes to high cliffs, then to marsh and fen. Once again, there has been continual change in the shape of the coast, with both flooding and reclamation. But this stretch of Norfolk's coastline is subtly different in many ways. Fluctuations in sea level have affected the regime of land use and habitation of this area throughout the millennia. The fenland, in particular, has been the continued subject of attempts at drainage and land reclamation.

Seaborne trade has been of particular importance here in historical times and probably in earlier times, too. International trade routes connected this coast with countries around the North Sea.

Archaeological sites situated in this area, both on and adjacent to the Deep History Coast, will enable us to look at the final prehistoric period. Here, we shall encounter some important settlements of the last episode of prehistory, which is the Iron Age.

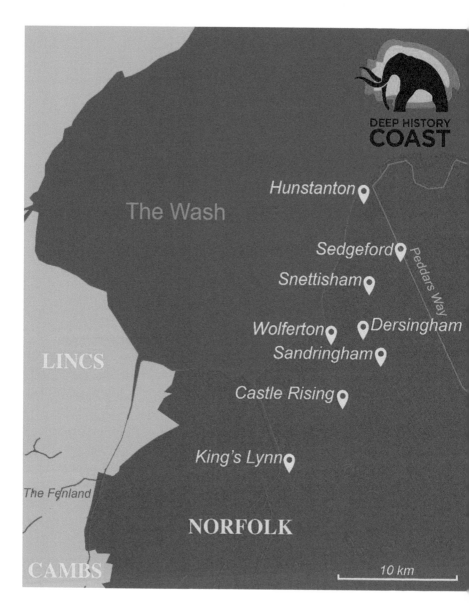

Fig. 49: The coast between Hunstanton and King's Lynn.

THE NORTH-WEST CORNER

The stretch of dunes that continues around Gore Point from Holme-next-the-Sea merges into cliffs at the northern extent of the town of Hunstanton. Here, one of the most distinctive and spectacular sites of the entire coastline can be enjoyed. Hunstanton's remarkable multicoloured cliffs rise prominently to some 20m in height and stand nearly vertical where they face the sea.

These cliffs are a unique location where the sequence of rocks that form Norfolk's solid geology can be seen. Their visually contrasting strata show the span of the Cretaceous period, as has been described in Chapter 3. The different layers provide evidence for changes in the Cretaceous sea level, reaching as far back in time as to about 112 million years ago.

Fig. 50: Hunstanton's distinctive red and white cliffs from beach level.

Fig. 51: Rectilinear blocks of upper Carstone at beach level, beneath the Hunstanton cliffs.

Fig. 52: Close-up of the formations known as Liesegang rings within the upper Carstone beneath Hunstanton cliffs.

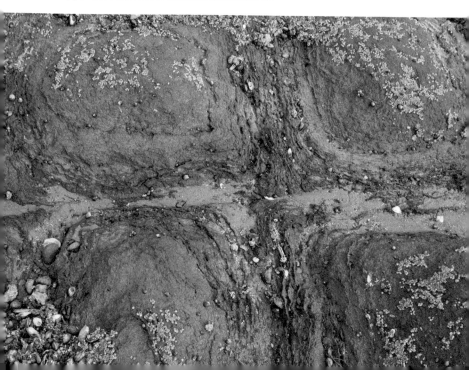

There are three main layers. At the bottom is Carstone, which is between 112 and 105 million years old. This is a brown iron-rich form of sandstone, which is closely associated with west Norfolk. It is frequently used in construction and is thus characteristic of the region's villages and buildings. Here in the cliff, it comprises yellow-brown, above red-brown and lower dark-brown layers.

Above the Carstone is red chalk. This distinctive layer is essentially the same as other chalk but its colouration is the result of its proximity to iron-rich deposits during its formation. The sequence is topped by white chalk. The lower, more brightly coloured layers are more fragile and are eroding on a steady basis, largely due to undercutting of the cliff and a resulting collapse of the upper chalk.

This is an excellent location for fossil hunting. Ammonites, belemnites and burrow trace fossils are present in the red layer. Tumbled cliff material spreads along the cliff side of the beach. Fossils can be found inside the chunks of both red limestone and white chalk.

On the beach beneath the cliff is another striking landscape. A series of grey-brown Carstone outcrops have been eroded by the sea into a rectilinear, grid-shaped formation. Each separate block carries a curious square-shaped feature known as a Liesegang ring, which was created by percolating water from the adjacent joints and bedding planes.

HUNSTANTON

As we approach the town of Hunstanton, we first reach the Old Town, which sits back behind the clifftop. The New Town starts further along the cliff and descends south and towards the sea.

Hunstanton today is a prominent seaside resort, popular with day trippers. It became favoured as a place for bathing during the mid-nineteenth century and was boosted by the arrival of the railway in 1862. It grew further in the late nineteenth and early twentieth centuries. It is still characterised by its Victorian and

Edwardian architecture and design, which extend along clifftop promenades.

In 1970, road building at Redgate Hill, to the south of the New Town, revealed evidence for another prehistoric presence. Excavation uncovered remains of a Neolithic and Early Bronze Age settlement. There were numerous post holes, representing structures, together with a large enclosure and a circular hut of Early Bronze Age date.

Just 1km on the landward side of the town, at Ringstead Downs, can be found another remnant of the region's glacial past. Most easily accessed from the delightful village of Ringstead is an area of rolling chalk grassland, which is now a Norfolk Wildlife Trust nature reserve. Here, it is possible to walk through a steep-sided dry valley that was formed as a glacial overflow channel. It was originally carved out of the chalk by glacial meltwaters, during the last glaciation, about 14,000 years ago.

Fig. 53: The dry valley at Ringstead Downs, formed by glacial meltwaters over 14,000 years ago.

THE WASH

The cliffs and beach at Hunstanton provide a splendid vantage point from which to observe the massive bay and estuary called the Wash. The coastline of far-off Lincolnshire can be observed just above the horizon and this is a perfect place from which to watch the most dramatic of sunsets, as the fading light plays onto the westward-facing multicoloured cliffs. The east coast of the Wash extends due south to the mouth of the River Great Ouse at King's Lynn and the start of the fenland.

In ecological terms, this part of the coast is one of the most important wetlands in Europe. The edges of the Wash provide a range of habitats, including salt marsh, tidal mudflats, shallow waters and deep channels where wading birds thrive. It is renowned for its clouds of birds, which can cover the sky; in particular, those of knot and redshank.

This expanse of water stretches westwards for 20km towards Lincolnshire and further south for 30km below Hunstanton. It opens northward into the North Sea. Its shape was originally gouged out by ice during the Wolstonian and Devensian stages of the Ice Age. When the ice finally retreated, the rivers Great Ouse, Welland and Nene flowed into the depression. This is now the largest estuary system in the whole of Great Britain.

Recent surveys of the sea floor are revealing detailed information about the part of the lost landscape of Doggerland that lies beyond the Wash. A large trench, some 20km north of the current coast at this point, has been identified and extends north-westward for some 50km. Core sampling has shown that this was once a large river valley within a tide-dominated estuary, before the flooding of Doggerland. It is known as the Southern River Valley.

Inland, the landscape beside the Wash is low lying and today provides rich arable farming. The shoreline itself has supported a specialised coastal industry of fishing, trade and associated activities, which have endured for thousands of years.

Fig. 54: The view from Snettisham beach, looking out across the Wash.

On its southern edges and across parts of the adjacent fenland, conditions enabled salt production, which was undertaken from prehistoric, through Roman and Anglo-Saxon times. At every high tide, the water at these fen-edge sites would flood a network of natural streams and creeks that ran up to several miles inland. It was then directed into a series of artificial ditches and tanks, where it was allowed to settle. Then it was ladled into pottery troughs, set over peat fires. The water evaporated, leaving salt crystals behind. Fragments of these troughs are found regularly at many locations along Norfolk's fen edge. Roman salt production sites have been excavated at Denver, Middleton and Blackborough End, which produced the largest assemblage of material from a Roman saltern in East Anglia.

TOWARDS SNETTISHAM

The high cliffs at the northern end of Hunstanton give way to sandy beaches below the town, which extend southwards, through and beyond Heacham, just 3 miles from Hunstanton. Heacham is another seaside town. A unique tourist attraction there is Norfolk Lavender, a lavender farm and gardens that was founded in 1932 and holds the national collection for the plant.

Heacham's wide, sandy beach gives way to mudflats at Snettisham, beyond Shepherd's Port, where there is a small seaside resort at the edge of the Wash. This is another area of outstanding natural beauty. The beach, including sandflats and mudflats, is home to large numbers of seabirds and waders. This is also the best place to view murmurations of seabirds. An RSPB reserve is situated to the south of Shepherd's Port. It contains a line of gravel pits, which form lagoons and provide attractive roosts for waders. It is situated just to the south-west of the dominant natural feature of raised hilltop that contains Ken Hill.

Fig. 55: The view towards Ken Hill, Snettisham, from the shoreside lagoons.

KEN HILL AND THE IRON AGE IN THE WEST

Snettisham will now be a more familiar name to people through the interventions of the BBC *Springwatch* team. The location of Wild Ken Hill has become a favoured location for the popular television series, as mentioned in Chapter 4. However, Ken Hill has been a special location for a very long period of time, reaching back into prehistory.

The raised topography at Snettisham's Ken Hill is an ideal point from which to introduce the final phase of prehistoric Norfolk, which we call the Iron Age. The start of that period in northern East Anglia dates from about 700 BC and lasted to the middle of the first century AD and the Roman conquest. The transition from the preceding Bronze Age saw the steadily increasing use of iron, alongside the continued working of bronze. By this time, substantial woodland clearance was under way and the landscape was being farmed intensively. As the population increased, management and control of the land was becoming important.

Several sites located in west Norfolk, and in proximity to the coast, came to prominence during the first century BC. The most well-known of these is at Ken Hill itself, which has seen human activity since the Bronze Age, and perhaps even earlier. During the Late Iron Age, it became a focus for the burial of precious metalwork objects, notably hoards of the elaborate gold and silver neck rings that we call torcs.

Ken Hill is situated 2km inland on the northern end of the prominent hilltop above Snettisham village, dominating the coastline and surrounding landscape of north-west Norfolk. The Iron Age site was located at the highest point and provided views right across the Wash, into Lincolnshire, as well as far inland. It would, in turn, have been highly visible for many miles around, across land and sea, which was possibly of even greater significance.

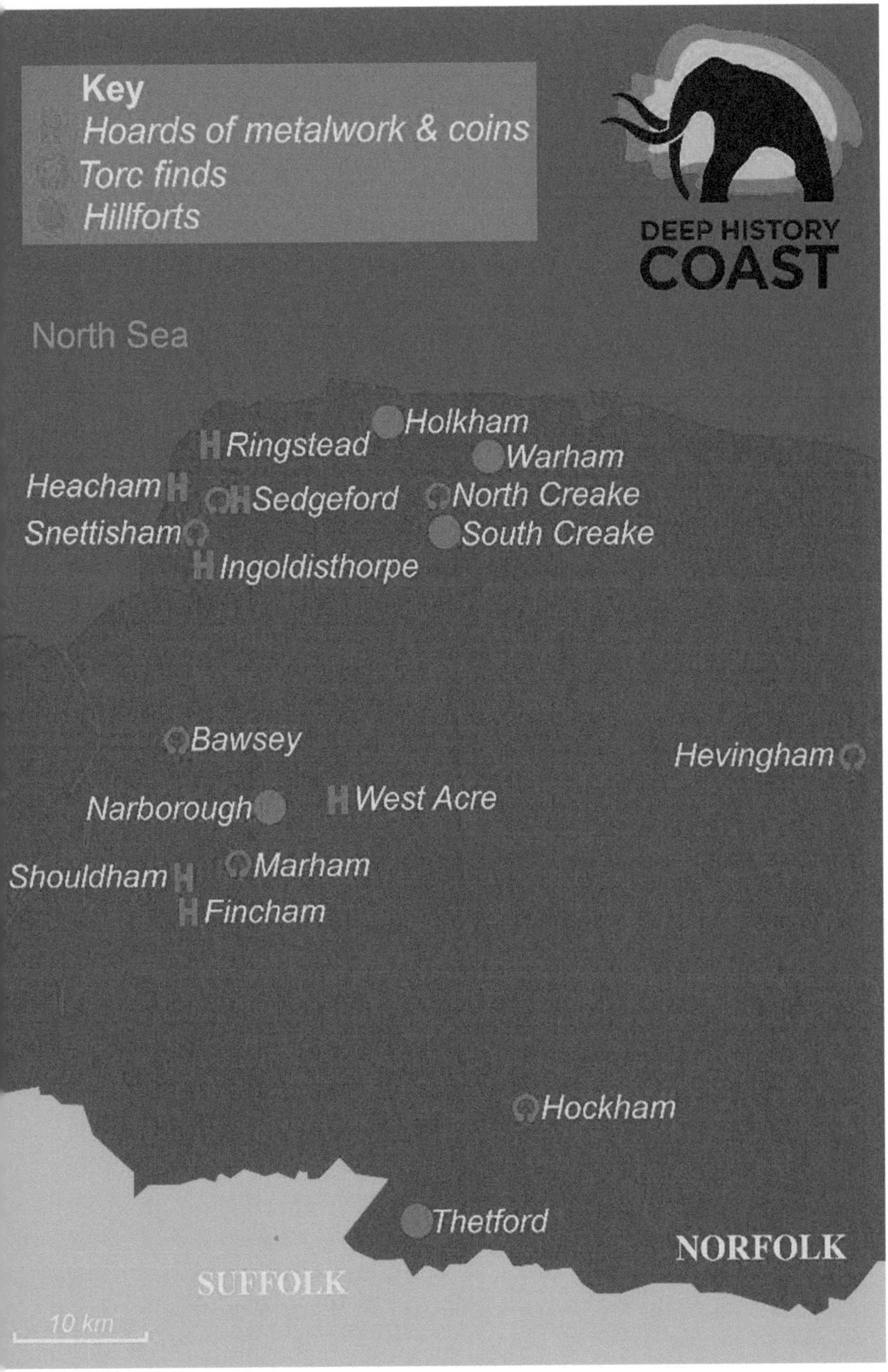

ig. 56: Locations of Iron Age hoards, torcs and hillforts.

The discovery of precious metalwork was initially made there in 1948. Subsequent excavations have revealed gold, silver and bronze torcs, rings, coins and other metalwork. This was a concentration of enormous wealth, both in ancient, as well as in modern terms. Some finds provide evidence for contact with the Mediterranean world, with coins from Carthage (north Africa), Gaul (France) and Greece, as well as other parts of Britain. This suggests that there could have been an ancient trading port in the near vicinity, perhaps located on the Wash, adjacent to Snettisham or maybe further north in the Brancaster area. This exceptionally rich site may have been a ritual and religious focus of international renown.

Other Iron Age Sites in the West

Another prominent Late Iron Age site in west Norfolk was at nearby Sedgeford, situated just 2km inland from Heacham. Sedgeford is a small village, again located in a high position. An annual campaign of excavation and surveys since 1996 by the Sedgeford Historical and Archaeological Research Project (SHARP) has again provided evidence for a significant Iron Age presence.

Further south, and just to the east of King's Lynn at Bawsey is another site that has revealed exceptional finds of Iron Age date. It was originally situated in a prominent and visible location on a peninsula above the Gay River estuary. Finds recorded since 1941 include more electrum and gold torcs, torc terminals and decorative pieces of horse harness.

Iron Age torcs are rare finds in Britain. More have been discovered in East Anglia than in the whole of the rest of the country, with most of them coming from west Norfolk. The greatest concentration was at Ken Hill, while others have come from North Creake and Marham, as well as Sedgeford and Bawsey; all within just 7km of the Deep History Coast and the fen edge. Although the significance of this buried wealth is not fully understood, it is clear that west and coastal Norfolk had a special significance during this final phase of British prehistory.

Iron Age Hillforts in Norfolk

A form of late prehistoric site more often found in higher parts of Britain but also associated with west Norfolk is that popularly referred to as hillforts. These earthworks are all broadly circular or oval in shape, surrounded by ditches and located at prominent natural positions in the landscape. Although Norfolk's hillforts have not been closely dated, they all appear to have been constructed during the Iron Age. This group of sites, in general, represent some of the earliest permanent settlements used by the wider community, although our understanding of the Norfolk examples remains very slight.

Examples are known at Holkham, Warham Camp, South Creake and Narborough; all within just 10km of the coastline or the fen edge. As a group, they are set just inland from and close to the other prominent and rich Iron Age sites mentioned above. The first three are readily visitable and Warham, in particular, contains well-preserved banks and ditches, coupled with spectacular views of the countryside.

KING'S LYNN AND ITS SURROUNDING AREA

As we move down the coast of the Wash from Snettisham to the south of Shepherd's Port and seaward of the RSPB reserve, Wolferton Creake leads to the charming village of Wolferton, 6km south of Snettisham. The coastline adjacent to the Wash has changed significantly since its early formation. The process of longshore drift has caused the build-up of land at its edge and places that were once on the coast are now located inland. Here at Wolferton can be found a high cliff that once defined the coastline but now lies 2.5km inland. Fine views towards the current coast can be enjoyed from here.

Situated immediately to the east of Wolferton is the Sandringham Estate, where a royal connection is held in special affection by the people of the county. Sandringham has been the private home for four generations of British monarchs. King George V (1865–1936) called it 'the place I love better than anywhere else in the world'. It is also where King George VI (1895–1952) died. Today's royal family traditionally spend the winter months there and it is from where the late Queen Elizabeth II would broadcast to the nation each Christmas.

Further south is the village of Castle Rising, which had an early medieval origin, including a planned street layout associated with its Norman church and castle. Now situated some 6km inland, the settlement had originally developed as a port on the River Babingley, which was then directly navigable from the Wash.

The main urban centre in west Norfolk is King's Lynn, which was another new town created under the Normans and was originally called Bishop's Lynn. Its importance grew as a result of its location on the Wash, on a sea route enabling North Sea trade. The town's foundation has been attributed to Herbert Losinga, first Bishop of Norwich, although there was already occupation associated with the thriving salt-making industry around the Wash. Bishop's Lynn was given a charter by King John in 1204.

Fig. 57: The former coastal cliff at Wolferton, now situated 3km inland.

Lynn remained one of the country's richest ports throughout the medieval period. International trade linked the town with Iceland, Russia, Germany, Venice and Gascony in France. Its whaling fleet sailed to Greenland every spring. Lynn also traded with all other parts of England.

In 1241, the German cities of Hamburg and Lubeck united to form a trading alliance that maintained a major impact across the North Sea world for some 500 years. Known as the Hanseatic League, it became an international association of towns and ports for trading purposes. Lynn's coastal situation made it ideally situated to join the league, becoming Britain's first member in the late thirteenth century.

In 1536, the town ceased to be under the protection of the Bishops of Norwich. King Henry VIII claimed Lynn and what had been Bishop's Lynn became King's Lynn. It has remained an important market town serving west Norfolk and the eastern fens.

The historic character and status of the town are preserved in a wealth of buildings, which trace its development over 1,000 years. Part of the medieval town wall survives, together with the remains of four monasteries, merchants' houses, warehouses and the Customs House of 1683. The remarkable fifteenth-century South Gate is still a fittingly grand entry point. Other notable buildings include the Churches of St Margaret and St Nicholas, and the fifteenth-century Guildhall of St George, resplendent in its chequered flint-and-stone facing.

THE FENLAND

To the south of King's Lynn, the landscape becomes completely flat as we enter the fenland, which is situated along the southern edges of the Wash. Highly atmospheric, with big skies and dramatic cloudscapes, the fens cover parts of the counties of Lincolnshire and Cambridgeshire, as well as 200 square miles of south-west Norfolk. This is a naturally marshy area and supports a rich ecology. This very distinct environment also serves to lessen the effect of extreme weather conditions that erode other parts of the county's exposed coastline.

At the end of the last ice age, the natural drainage flowed northward (see above), across the area that is now west Norfolk, into the depression left by the ice sheets. As the ice melted and the sea level rose, water covered the former land surface and formed the fenland, with a coastline that we would broadly recognise today. The fens developed into an extensive area of reed swamp and marshland vegetation. As the waters became increasingly stagnant, dead plant material was unable to rot in the oxygen-free conditions and peat began to form.

The formation of the fen peat stimulated the growth of trees. The landscape developed into one of wetlands and forest. Natural resources were diverse and abundant and included fish, fowl and game, together with reeds and thatch, which provided an attractive habitat for people.

Human exploitation of the fenland has responded to changing sea levels over the millennia. Some small islands that projected above the peat and around the edge originally provided a favourable landscape for settlement, from early post-glacial times. The first people were attracted by the rich natural resources. They were initially restricted to the higher locations but then clearance of the forest revealed the benefits of the rich peaty soils. Specialist lifestyles developed as they learned to maintain the watery environment with its ditches and dykes and exploit the wildfowl, game, fish and eels.

Settlements of the Neolithic and Bronze Age have been found buried beneath the peat. In particular, significant amounts of Bronze Age metalwork have been discovered around the fen edge. This location appears to have favoured settlement, and by that time, the people were raising domesticated animals, including cattle, sheep and goats for milk, meat and leather. At one site in the south-eastern fenland, a remarkable collection of Middle Bronze Age metalwork items has been discovered at Methwold, revealing what had been a significant occupation site. Metalwork recovered belonged to the earlier part of the Middle Bronze Age, between about 1500–1300 BC.

The fens have frequently flooded during winter months and have been subject to continued attempts at drainage in more recent historical times. It was the Romans who recognised the agricultural potential of the rich peaty soils and they made efforts to drain areas. However, the most significant changes did not occur until many centuries later. It was in the early seventeenth century that the advantages of introducing dykes, dams and sluices in order to provide proper drainage to improve the productivity of this naturally fertile landscape was understood. Drainage of the southern peat fens was achieved between 1630 and 1653 under the Dutch engineer Cornelius Vermuyden. The improvements continued through to the late seventeenth century, creating what has become some of the best agricultural land in England.

9. ACCESSING AND LEARNING FROM THE DEEP HISTORY COAST

HOW YOU CAN ACCESS AND ENJOY NORFOLK'S DEEP HISTORY COAST

Having explored the landscape, geology and early archaeology of Norfolk's coastline, we look at how people can become involved and enjoy this unique landscape in different ways. Visitors to the county are encouraged to experience the fascinating archaeological and geological sites of the Deep History Coast. These places are all found in atmospheric rural locations, set within areas of outstanding natural beauty. But there are many other ways in which people can enjoy and become involved in the wonders of this coastline. In this chapter we shall share some ideas.

THE BEACHES

As has been shown in the preceding chapters, Norfolk's beaches range across a variety of environments and offer so many different activities for visitors. Some might be those most suitable for young people, such as for flying a kite or ball sports. Most of Norfolk's beaches are sandy and perfect for building sandcastles and sand sculptures. Responsible rockpooling is a wonderful way of providing an introduction to some of the smaller living creatures that share our natural world.

Other activities might include watching seabirds. Their variety and diversity in the range of habitats is special to Norfolk. Or you might enjoy walking – or even simply relaxing on the beach.

Beachcombing

The beaches of the Deep History Coast are particularly interesting for searching and a patient beachcomber will discover many things to identify and learn more about. A walk on the beach after severe weather can often be very rewarding. The first remains of the West Runton mammoth were discovered in this way.

Each item found can be examined and identified. There are four main categories of common finds on the beach:

- fossils, such as belemnites and echinoids, from about 80 million years ago, and fragments of bone, antler and tusk from about 700,000 years ago
- pebbles, such as flint, chalk, clay ironstones and erratics (a rock that has come from elsewhere)
- semi-precious stones, such as amber, jasper, carnelian and jet
- finds of more recent origin such as shells, cuttlefish bones, bryozoa, seaweeds, whelk egg-cases and mermaids' purses.

Amber

Amber is a fossil resin from several species of pine tree in the family Sciadopityaceae, which grew in Europe about 44 million years ago (during the Eocene Epoch). Worldwide, they are now all extinct except for one species that survives in Japan – the Japanese umbrella pine (*Sciadopitys verticillata*). The most significant amber-bearing deposits are on the Baltic coasts of Russia, Bulgaria, Lithuania and Poland.

Fragments of amber are sometimes washed up on the Norfolk coast by the sea, usually after easterly winds, and can be mixed with tiny aquatic invertebrate animals called bryozoa and seaweed thrown up by spring gales. This amber was transported from the

Baltic Region by westerly flowing rivers during the ice ages and deposited all over Western Europe. Old river deposits now lying under the North Sea are sometimes disturbed during gales and pieces of ancient amber can float to the surface.

Amber is one of the few varieties of organic gemstone. The most common varieties of organic gems include amber, pearl and coral. Unlike most other coloured stones, amber has an amorphous rather than crystalline structure. It has a very low specific gravity, which means that it is exceptionally light. Its low density allows it to float in salt water.

Amber's formation process began with the transformation of tree resin into what is called copal. This change was triggered when overlying sediments created high pressure and raised temperatures. The exposure to heat and pressure repelled organic compounds called terpenes, which can cause deterioration and decay. Over time, the resin eventually hardened and became fossilised amber.

Many trees produce resin today, as well as in the past, but most do not actually produce amber. Most resin deposits degrade after prolonged exposure to sunlight, rain and extreme temperatures. However, umbrella-pine resin is very resilient and resistant to decay.

Amber can contain insects, spiders and other invertebrates, and even sometimes small lizards and other vertebrates. They became trapped in the resin when it was oozing down the trunks of ancient pine trees.

Because of its softness and colour, amber has long been carved into ornaments and jewellery. In Norfolk, amber beads have been found that were carved at least 3,600 years ago.

On Norfolk's Deep History Coast, amber can be found at places such as Cromer beach, although larger quantities turn up at other locations, such as Southwold in Suffolk.

Genuine amber can easily be confused with several other similar-looking materials. Carnelian (sometimes spelled cornelian) is a brownish-red or amber-coloured mineral commonly used as a semi-precious gemstone. Carnelian is a variety of the mineral chalcedony, coloured by impurities of iron oxides. It is frequently found on Norfolk's beaches, but it is hard, cold to the touch and will not float in sea water.

Unfortunately, synthetic resins and plastics can be found on our beaches too, and if discoloured, they can look very much like real amber. Unlike natural carnelians, they are often as soft as amber, are warmer to touch and will float in sea water. Here are two simple ways to tell if a substance is real amber, or a synthetic material:

- The substance can be warmed up by rubbing it with a cloth or your hands. Real amber has a faint resinous odour resembling pine or turpentine. Synthetics will give out a chemical smell.
- A hot needle can be touched on the surface of the object. Artificial materials will give off an unpleasant smell, whereas natural amber smells of pine, rosin or incense.

Searching for Fossils

The discovery, collection and study of fossils is called Palaeontology. An introduction to Norfolk's fossils has been provided in Chapter 3. Collecting is fun and exciting and gives us the chance to find out for ourselves about the Deep History of our planet. However, we must keep in mind that there are only a limited number of fossils in existence. Most visitors are very responsible in the way they fossil hunt and leave enough for others to find as well. Make sure you are a responsible fossil collector by following the guidelines below:

- Stick to the footpaths provided. Do not add to coastal erosion by trying to climb up or down the cliffs.
- Never dig into the cliffs as it can add to erosion, is dangerous and spoils things for others. There are plenty of fossils on the beach anyway. Much of Norfolk's Deep History Coast is a Site of Special Scientific Interest (SSSI), so in many cases it is illegal to dig into the cliffs.

- Take only a few representative specimens from the beach.
- Always make a note of where you find fossils, as they might be important. Photographs can be very helpful.
- Write a label for your fossils, including exactly where and when they were collected, plus any other observations.
- Large fossils can be problematic for individual collectors to move. It may be better to leave them for others to see. Otherwise, seek advice or help from the local museum.
- Avoid disturbing wildlife.
- Remember that fossil sites are for everyone to enjoy and indiscriminate collecting will damage this resource for future visitors.

Palaeontological Preparation: Best Practice

Norfolk's Deep History Coast is one of the best places in the country to find fossils. Those who come across these palaeontological treasures should be aware that there is some strange and outdated information available on what to do with them once you have found them. The following advice should prove helpful.

One commonly heard urban myth is that the best way to get rid of salt from fossils found on the coast it to leave them in your toilet cistern! Certainly, submerging salt-saturated fossils in toilet water does get rid of salts, but the abrupt change from salt to fresh water can also lead to problems, while drying and cracking and increased fragility can be an issue further down the line. In fact, some fossils found on the Deep History Coast don't have any salt in them anyway, so gradual drying (nowhere near a radiator or other heat source) is the best way to preserve them.

If a fossil is found below the tideline on the beach and it starts to show a whitish, powdery layer on its surface as it begins to dry, then it probably does have salt in it from seawater. Outlined below is the best way to deal with salty fossils – using a saline or salt 'ladder':

- Fully submerge the fossil in water as salty as the sea (tap water is fine with six teaspoons of salt per litre).
- After a couple of days, change the water so that it is less salty (five teaspoons). Keep doing this every couple of days until you are using pure water. This will make sure all the salts are leached out and you won't get as many problems down the line.
- Dry it out slowly (not next to a radiator); again, over a number of days or weeks.

In the 1980s and early 1990s it was common practice to use PVA (polyvinyl acetate) glue to consolidate (stabilise) and fix broken fossils, even in specialised museums. This was because, at the time, there was nothing readily available that was better. However, the product hadn't been tested for what might happen decades into the future and we now know that PVA can damage fossils. They will yellow over time and it can be very difficult to remove. More recently, professional organisations such as museums use acrylic resins instead of PVA to fix breaks in fossils, as well as in ceramics and glass. It is reversable, durable, non-yellowing and stable over long periods of time. However, for home use, it isn't really appropriate, as such chemicals can be harmful if used incorrectly. Always seek professional advice before attempting to glue or fix any fossils.

In the past, plumbers' epoxy putty was used by amateurs and professionals alike to fill large missing areas in fossils. This unforgiving material dries extremely hard, doesn't expand and contract, and is almost impossible to remove without damaging the fossil.

Most fossils are fine left as they are, and gaps in them can actually help us to see aspects of their anatomy that might be difficult to spot if there wasn't a hole there. Others can be stored slightly apart in such a way that suggests the missing piece. If you absolutely have to fill a gap in a fossil, then do seek professional advice.

In the main, fossils from the Deep History Coast are stable once they have dried out. Avoid sudden changes in temperature and humidity and keep them away from direct heat (such as radiators, stoves or fireplaces) and they should last indefinitely. However, if there is a sudden change in temperature, they may crack. If there is a change in humidity, then some fossils (especially those from the Cromer Forest-Bed Formation) can suffer from 'pyrite rot'. This sounds like a nasty disease, but it is in fact a real problem in fossils. It is where stable iron minerals decay with exposure to moisture in the air to become brittle, yellow iron sulphate. This shows up as a crumbly, bright-yellow powdery substance that smells like rotten eggs. The best cure is prevention, and if your fossils are stored in a low-humidity environment (such as in the house, not in a shed or damp garage), then they should be fine.

If your fossils are kept in a stable environment – not too damp and not too cold or warm, and especially without any sudden changes in humidity or temperature – they should last forever.

VISITING HISTORIC SITES

Many people will visit the Deep History Coast to experience the very early prehistoric sites. But there are also opportunities to enjoy other places of later historical significance. This coastal region has a rich and unique legacy covering all historical periods. There are many fascinating buildings constructed from Roman and medieval times through to the present day. Roman sites include visitable Saxon Shore forts, as mentioned in previous chapters. A large number of medieval churches and castles also provide a wonderful source of interest for visitors.

As well as buildings, there are country parks, including those at Felbrigg, Holkham, Sandringham and Sheringham, with their own historical importance. They do also contain a wealth of later historic buildings together with open grounds for recreation and country walks.

VISIT THE MUSEUMS

Norfolk is well served by museums, which reflect all aspects of life in the county and its past. It is possible to visit a diverse range of collections and archives. The sites of the Norfolk Museums Service in particular possess collections and information related to Norfolk's Deep History Coast.

Time and Tide Museum, Great Yarmouth
Time and Tide occupies the premises of the Tower Fish Curing Works, originally built in 1850. The museum tells the story of Great Yarmouth and contains displays on the early archaeology of the area.

Cromer Museum
Located in Victorian fishermen's cottages, the museum has a gallery devoted to local geology with an amazing collection of fossils and information about the Deep History Coast and the West Runton mammoth.

The Lynn Museum
This museum tells the story of King's Lynn. It has a permanent exhibition related to Seahenge and displays the timbers and central stump. There are also good collections of other prehistoric objects.

Norfolk Collections Centre, Farm and Workhouse, Gressenhall
The Norfolk Collections Centre is the NMS's access storage facility, housing over 3 million objects. Among the objects in store are the bones of the West Runton mammoth. Look out for special tour dates, where everything from the history of brewing in Norfolk to tours focusing on the mammoth itself can be booked.

Norwich Castle Museum and Study Centre
This is the flagship county museum. Its collections cover the county of Norfolk, its history, culture and environment. The famous Happisburgh handaxe is displayed here.

There are other independent museums located on the coast, which include:

The Museum of the Broads at Stalham
This museum tells the history of the Norfolk and Suffolk Broads.

The Henry Blogg Museum, Cromer
A museum that tells the story of the local north-coast lifeboats and their crews.

Sheringham Museum
This museum covers the history of the town and its maritime associations.

The Muckleburgh Collection at Weybourne
This is a military museum set on the coast, with one of the largest private collections of military vehicles in the country.

USE THE COASTAL TRAILS

The whole of Norfolk's coast can be enjoyed on foot or by bicycle. There are many dedicated walks that converge on this area.

The Norfolk Coast Path stretches from Cromer to Holme-next-the-Sea, where it joins with the Peddars Way. This route, which was mentioned in the previous chapter, can be followed for 46 miles, from Holme-next-the-Sea and running south, through north Norfolk and Breckland, eventually to Knettishall, east of Thetford.

Fig. 58: Norfolk Coast Path signs.

Fig. 59: A Deep History Coast 'discovery point' at West Runton.

Further to the east, the Paston Way starts at Cromer and runs east along the coast, before turning inland to North Walsham. From there, the Weavers' Way runs through Broadland, finishing at Great Yarmouth.

There are a number of cycle routes, which include the North Norfolk Coast Cycleway. Most of the Peddars Way is also accessible to cyclists.

Deep History Coast Discovery and Information Points have been created across north Norfolk. They can be found at locations between Weybourne and Cart Gap, between Happisburgh and Eccles.

WILDLIFE AND CONSERVATION

A popular activity is to focus on the unique diversity of wildlife that can be found along the coast. In particular, Norfolk is generally considered to be the top county in the UK for birdwatching, which can be enjoyed from any location on the coast.

Norfolk's coast projects into the North Sea, where many bird species make landfall on their migrations from Europe and Scandinavia. On Norfolk's Deep History Coast, they enjoy the diverse range of watery habitats, especially the large stretches of salt marsh and the extensive estuarine mudflats adjacent to the Wash. The soft eroding cliffs of the Deep History Coast provide a habitat for a diverse range of invertebrates, as well as for nesting birds such as sand martins. A colony of seals can be watched at Horsey beach on the east coast and boat trips to view those resident at Blakeney depart from Morston.

There are bird and nature reserves, including those at Hickling Broad, Cley Marshes, Salthouse Marshes, Holkham, Titchwell, Holme Dunes, Dersingham, Welney and Pensthorpe, near Fakenham. In this way, Norfolk is playing an important role in wildlife and habitat conservation. Indeed, Norfolk Wildlife Trust was the very first of the wildlife trusts, being set up in 1926 when 435 acres of Cley Marshes were purchased to be preserved 'as a bird-breeding sanctuary for all time'.

OUTDOOR PURSUITS AND WATER SPORTS

Outdoor physical activities can be enjoyed in appropriate places along the coastline. These including swimming and other forms of water sports. As well as surfing, action sports include the increasingly popular kiteboarding, or kitesurfing, which embraces elements of windsurfing, paragliding and sailing.

Angling has always been a popular pastime in Norfolk and is long associated with the popular local TV presenter and fishing writer, the late John Wilson. Sea-fishing trips from the Norfolk coast are still increasing in popularity. Crabbing from Cromer Pier is also a popular free activity for families visiting the area as well as with the locals.

However, many people still prefer walking. Dog walkers are always the most abundant visitors on all parts of the coast.

AN ARTIST'S PARADISE

From the nineteenth century to the present day, artists have drawn inspiration from the Norfolk landscape. It has been the coast, in particular, that has attracted large numbers. The Norwich Society of artists was founded in 1803 by John Crome and his friend Robert Ladbrooke. It brought together professional and amateur painters, becoming the first regional school of painting in England.

Other members of 'the Norwich School' were John Sell Cotman, George Vincent, James Stark, Joseph and Alfred Stannard, John Thirtle, Thomas Lound and Henry Ninham. Their work was based on realism and was derived from direct observation of the local landscape. They found their inspiration in the local heaths, woodland and rivers, as well as from the Norfolk coast. From about 1828, the subjects of sea, sky and shore took on a special significance for the group.

Today, the arts are generally well served on the coast. In addition to communities of artists, there are many galleries situated in towns on the coast and slightly inland.

COASTAL CUISINE

There is a distinctive cuisine associated with Norfolk's coast. As well as fresh fish, its shellfish include Cromer crabs, Brancaster mussels, shrimps from the Wash, cockles from Stiffkey and oysters from Thornham, Blakeney and Brancaster. There are artisan cheeses, while the finest malting barley comes from north Norfolk.

Spikey, green, leafless stalks of samphire are scoured from the salt marshes. This increasingly popular vegetable is sometimes referred to as sea asparagus and is now considered a local delicacy. It is best eaten steamed and with butter.

There are many outstanding and diverse restaurants in the towns and villages. This is not to overlook the ever-popular fish and chip shops to be found in towns and villages right along the coast.

CONTRIBUTE TO ARCHAEOLOGY IN NORFOLK

Many archaeological discoveries are made by chance, by people walking in the landscape and along the beaches and cliffs. It is not always apparent what the finds are or how important they might turn out to be. Fortunately, the public are encouraged to show and report their discoveries to NMS and the staff of the Identification and Recording Service, who are always pleased to identify new finds.

Today, more archaeological finds are made in Norfolk than in any other county and most of them by the general public. As a result, there has been a transformation in our understanding of our past. Our growing historical records provide a rich resource for the better understanding of all archaeological periods. You too can make a difference if you report your finds. This process has been responsible for many discoveries that have enabled us to realise the significance of Norfolk's Deep History Coast.

THE FUTURE

Today, the effects of climate change and global warming are already being felt in our increasingly erratic weather conditions. Through the progressive warming of our planet, we are once again experiencing the melting of ice sheets and facing a global rise in sea levels. We have seen that the geological record shows how the earth has undergone such changing conditions in the past.

The study of our past provides a warning for the future of humankind in the face of immensely powerful natural forces. It also poses the question of whether we can be as resilient as our predecessors as we struggle to ensure the survival of our planet and life as we know it, as we are once again faced with the consequences of climate change.

This exploration of Norfolk's coastline has revealed insights into our human past and the lives and character of our distant relatives. It enables us to address new questions as to why people chose to travel huge distances to experience more demanding environments. What routes did they use to come north? And how did they survive these harsher conditions so long ago? As we seek the answers to such questions, it will serve to enhance our understanding of human behaviour.

The study of our early history and prehistory shows the fragility, as well as the resilience, of our species against the background of a dynamic and sometimes hostile landscape and climate. The climatic fluctuations of the Ice Age, in particular, were responsible for extinctions of human life, leading to subsequent recolonisations. In fact, the present span of occupation in Britain by *Homo sapiens* has been for less than just 12,000 years. The loss of Doggerland then resulted in a reduction in the migrating animal species that could be exploited. The evidence being revealed on Norfolk's Deep History Coast has enabled us to trace the human response to such changes in the landscape and transient subsistence resources over past millennia.

The study of the Deep History Coast has also served to highlight the steady loss of species and an ongoing threat to biodiversity. *Homo sapiens* have been responsible for the extinction of many species and, in particular, the larger native fauna (megafauna). They have also influenced the evolution of some species, including the domesticated creatures familiar to us today. At the same time, they have created a range of new environments associated with human activity that have enabled other species to adapt and exploit new niches within the evolving landscape.

A fuller awareness and appreciation of what we have called Norfolk's Deep History Coast can help us towards a better understanding of the impact of human actions and the importance of preserving and cherishing what remains of our fragile natural environment. One of the attractions of this coast is its relative quiet and peaceful setting, but in the future we must achieve a balance through which we can protect it, while still encouraging its wider appreciation.

New discoveries are happening along Norfolk's coast regularly. More significant new finds will have been made there even since we started to write this book. People, by whom we include the public, archaeologists and workers such as those engaged in the offshore and fishing industries, are steadily revealing more evidence of our past. We are also studying and reassessing our existing important museum collections. At the same time, scientific research, employing new techniques, is making great advances in the fields of underwater surveying, methods of dating and the study of DNA. So, we are now able to learn even more from these discoveries than ever before.

The concept of Norfolk's Deep History Coast is an accessible way of conveying the importance and attraction of this area to more people. The name that we have created for the area is a broad term, which enables an appreciation of geology and nature, as well as history and archaeology. It can also embrace a broad chronology. In future, there remains the potential for adding the exploration of later historical periods, including the county's rich Anglo-Saxon, Viking and medieval archaeology.

The unfolding story of Norfolk's Deep History Coast will continue to have an increasing relevance to us all in many ways. It is a fragile environment, containing information of relevance to the progress and survival of humankind. We continue to learn from the study of how our earliest kin behaved in relation to the kind of threats we are facing once again in the twenty-first century.

What we do today echoes our response to climate change in the past and warns of the effect our modern lifestyle is having on our environment. We have witnessed how human populations chose to move south and north in response to cycles of climatic warming and cooling, which is no longer a realistic option in the modern world, and we are warned of the severity of the increasing threats to our planet. And the story emphatically shows that we are all ultimately one people, with common ancestors, who originated in East Africa 6 million years ago.

GLOSSARY

Ancient Human Occupation of Britain Project (AHOB):
This project ran between 2001–13. The director was Professor Chris Stringer of the Natural History Museum, London.

Barrier beach: A lengthy sand or shingle beach that runs parallel to the coast, separated by lagoons or salt marsh.

Bronze Age: The period from about 2500 BC to about 700 BC.

Crag: The Crag is made of layers of clays, muds, sands, gravels and pebbles, often cemented together by iron-rich sediments, generally, between about 2 and 5 million years old.

Cretaceous: The final period of the Mesozoic Era, from about 145 to 66 million years ago.

Deep Time: The very long expanses of time in relation to the development of the earth, when the rocks about us were formed.

Eocene: The geological epoch that lasted from about 56 million to nearly 34 million years ago.

Erratic: A rock or boulder that has been carried to a different location by glacial action.

Esker: A ridge formed from sands and gravels within a channel inside a glacier and deposited on the landscape.

Glacial outwash plain: A landscape formed at the terminus of a glacier by the action of meltwater and comprising sediments eroded from the underlying rocks.

Handaxe: A stone tool with a cutting edge, which is held in the hand and used for a range of purposes.

Haven: A navigable outlet to the sea.

Henge: A form of round enclosure of the later Neolithic or Bronze Age, consisting of a bank beyond an internal ditch.

Holocene: The current geological epoch, which began about 11,700 years ago.

Hominid: The larger family of primates, which includes the great apes.

Hominin: All modern and extinct human species, excluding the great apes.

Hunter-gatherers: Humans whose subsistence is derived from a combination of hunting wild animals, fishing and gathering edible wild plants and other natural foodstuffs.

Ichnotaxon: An ichnotaxon (plural ichnotaxa) is the name (or taxon) given to an organism or a group of organisms based purely on the fossilised evidence of that organism. Essentially, the name for a trace fossil, emulating the 'genus and species' system of the usual Linnaean taxonomy.

Iron Age: The period from about 700 BC to the Roman invasion of Britain in AD 43.

Kame: A mound formed from sands and gravels left by a retreating ice sheet.

Littoral drift: The longshore, seaborne transport of sediments, such as sands and gravels.

Macrofossil: A fossil that is visible to the naked eye.

Mantle: The mainly solid interior of the earth, between the core and the outer crust.

Megafauna: The large mammals of a particular region.

Mesolithic: The 'middle stone age'. The period from about 10,000 BC to about 4300 BC.

Neolithic: The 'new stone age'. The period from about 4300 BC to about 2500 BC.

Palaeolithic: The 'old stone age'. The period from the first presence of humans until approximately 10,000 BC.

Paramoudra: A large flint with a central cavity.

Plate tectonics: The theory that explains the structure of the earth's crust as resulting from the interaction of mobile plates floating above the earth's interior, or mantle.

Pleistocene: The first epoch of the Quaternary period, preceding the Holocene. From about 2.58 million to 11,700 years ago.

Raised beach: A former beach that is now situated above water level.

Ring ditch: A circular feature often revealed by aerial photography. It usually represents the ploughed-out remains of a Neolithic or Bronze Age round barrow burial monument.

Sea fret: A mist or fog coming in from the sea.

Stratigraphy: The order and relative position of geological deposits and layers of archaeological material in the ground.

Till: Unstratified sediments deposited by glacial action.

FURTHER READING

Ashton, N., *Early Humans* (William Collins, 2017).

Bottinelli, G. (ed.), *A Vision of England: Paintings of the Norwich School* (Norwich Castle Museum & Art Gallery, 2013).

Champion, M., *Seahenge: A Contemporary Chronicle* (Barnwell, 2000).

Clifford, E., and P. Bahn, *Everyday Life in the Ice Age* (Archaeopress, 2022).

Coles, B.J., 'Doggerland: a speculative survey', in *Proceedings of the Prehistoric Society*, 64, 45–81 (1998).

Dartnell, L., *Origins: How the Earth Shaped Human History* (Vintage, 2019).

Davies, J.A., *The Land of Boudica: Prehistoric and Roman Norfolk* (Heritage/Oxbow, 2009).

Davies, J.A., *The Little History of Norfolk* (The History Press, 2020).

Dinnis, R., and C. Stringer, *Britain: One Million Years of the Human Story* (Natural History Museum, 2013).

Dymond, D., *The Norfolk Landscape* (The Alastair Press, 1990).

Eyers, J., *Geology of the Norfolk Coast: Hunstanton to Happisburgh* (Chiltern Archaeology, 2021).

Fortey, R., *The Hidden Landscape: A Journey into the Geological Past* (Pimlico, 1993).

Gaffney, V., S. Fitch and D. Smith, *Europe's Lost World: The Rediscovery of Doggerland* (Council for British Archaeology, 2009).

Higham, T., *The World Before Us: How Science is Revealing a New Story of Our Human Origins* (Viking, 2021).

Holt-Wilson, T., *Norfolk's Earth Heritage – Valuing Our Geodiversity* (Norfolk Geodiversity Partnership, 2010).

Lister, A., *Mammoths: Ice Age Giants* (Natural History Museum, 2014).

Pestell, R., and D. Stannard, *Eccles-Juxta-Mare: A Lost Village Discovered* (Wortley, 1995).

Pettitt, P., and M. White, *The British Palaeolithic: Human Societies at the Edge of the Pleistocene World* (Routledge, 2012).

Pitts, M., and M. Roberts, *Fairweather Eden* (Arrow, 1998).

Roberts, A., *The Incredible Human Journey* (Bloomsbury, 2009).

Robinson, B., *The Nowhere Road: A Fresh Look at Norfolk's Peddars Way* (Elmstead, 2001).

Robinson, B., and M. Robinson, *Walking the Norfolk Long Distance Trail: The Coast Path* (Poppyland, 2006).

Rothe, T., *The Norfolk Coast, Book Two: Between Wolferton and Overstrand* (Pixz, 2011).

SHARP, *Digging Sedgeford: A People's Archaeology* (Poppyland, 2014).

Stringer, C., *Homo Britannicus* (Allen Lane, 2006).

Stuart, A.J., *Life in the Ice Age* (Shire, 1988).

Stuart, A.J., *The West Runton Elephant: Discovery and Excavation* (Norfolk Museums Service, 1997).

Watson, C., *Seahenge: An Archaeological Conundrum* (English Heritage, 2005).

Weston, C. and S., *Claimed by the Sea* (Wood Green, 1994).

Williamson, T., *England's Landscape: East Anglia* (English Heritage, 2006).

Yalden, D., *The History of British Mammals* (Poyser Natural History, 1999).